Badiou's Ontology of the Present

Also Available from Bloomsbury

Badiou and His Interlocutors (2018)
The Immanence of Truths (2022)
Understanding Badiou, Understanding Modernism (2024)

Badiou's Ontology of the Present

Society, Economy, and Culture in Transition

Michael Hauser
Translated by Melinda Reidinger

BLOOMSBURY ACADEMIC
LONDON • NEW YORK • OXFORD • NEW DELHI • SYDNEY

BLOOMSBURY ACADEMIC
Bloomsbury Publishing Plc, 50 Bedford Square, London, WC1B 3DP, UK
Bloomsbury Publishing Inc, 1359 Broadway, New York, NY 10018, USA
Bloomsbury Publishing Ireland, 29 Earlsfort Terrace, Dublin 2, D02 AY28, Ireland

BLOOMSBURY, BLOOMSBURY ACADEMIC and the Diana logo are trademarks of Bloomsbury Publishing Plc

First published in Great Britain 2026

Cover design by Charlotte Daniels
Cover image © Michael Hauser

A catalogue record for this book is available from the British Library.

Library of Congress Cataloging-in-Publication Data
Names: Hauser, Michael, 1972- author
http://id.loc.gov/authorities/names/no2009048088
Title: Badiou's ontology of the present : society, economy and culture in transition / Michael Hauser.
Description: 1. | London ; New York : Bloomsbury Academic, 2026. | Includes bibliographical references and index.
Identifiers: LCCN 2025021361 (print) | LCCN 2025021362 (ebook) | ISBN 9781350437845 hardback | ISBN 9781350437852 paperback | ISBN 9781350437876 epub | ISBN 9781350437869 pdf
Subjects: LCSH: Badiou, Alain http://id.loc.gov/rwo/agents/n82125750 | Social change–History–20th century | Social change–History–21st century | Neoliberalism http://id.loc.gov/authorities/subjects/sh2005001629 | Postmodernism http://id.loc.gov/authorities/subjects/sh85105557 | World politics–1989- http://id.loc.gov/authorities/subjects/sh90004173
Classification: LCC B2430.B274 H38 2025 (print) | LCC B2430.B274 (ebook)
LC record available at https://lccn.loc.gov/2025021361
LC ebook record available at https://lccn.loc.gov/2025021362

ISBN: HB: 978-1-3504-3784-5
PB: 978-1-3504-3785-2
ePDF: 978-1-3504-3786-9
eBook: 978-1-3504-3787-6

Typeset by Deanta Global Publishing Services, Chennai, India

Contents

Figures

Preface

The crisis consists precisely in the fact that the old is dying and the new cannot be born; in this interregnum a great variety of morbid symptoms appear.

—Antonio Gramsci

Why Do I Term the Present Period an Interregnum?

In 2012, Zygmunt Bauman published an essay that summarized the nature of planetary society, politics, and economics with the title "Times of Interregnum."[1] In it, he writes that we are experiencing the death of the "old order" and its three pillars—territory, state, and nation. Sovereignty is no longer territorial sovereignty, state sovereignty, or national sovereignty. Its nature is unanchored, "floating," and unclear. However, a new form of sovereignty is not yet in sight, as in our age there is a bewildering competition among many actors for a share in sovereignty. Multinational, commercial, and financial corporations gain economic power over nation-states, but the latter still retain a certain degree of sovereignty. There are no globally applied rules that would put limits on the demands for sovereignty pursued by individual actors, nor is there an institution or a political power that could limit those demands, nor is there an institution or political power that could effectively implement decisions at a planetary level. Uncertainty prevails concerning how far the influence of international, commercial, and financial corporations extends and how much sovereignty nation-states and the European Union have retained. This state of permanent uncertainty is caused by the rules and principles in politics, economics, and global relations in the twentieth century no longer applying, while new ones cannot emerge. Bauman terms this state an "interregnum"—a term that was lent its modern meaning by Antonio Gramsci in the 1930s. The original sense of the word was a transitional period between the death of one ruler and the beginning of his successor's reign. It was a period when people had the possibility to experience a certain interruption of monotonous government, law, and social order. Gramsci modified the meaning of this word and deepened it by using it to signify a period in which social and political processes are taking place in a state of crisis, creating a stalemate. On the one hand, they cause the disintegration and death of the given economic and political structures; on the other, they prevent the emergence of new structures. As Gramsci says, "the old is dying and the new cannot be born."

Other sociologists and political scientists have followed Bauman, using Gramsci's definition of the interregnum as an analytical framework for examining the processes that have been taking place over the last decade. The primary manifestations of the turmoil, riots, conflicts, and abrupt changes in the past few years have appeared at the political level with Brexit and the election of Donald Trump as the American president. The world order based on the hegemony of the United States is breaking down, but no new world order is on the horizon. Countless publications, debates, and events indicate that we are in a period of transition from a disintegrating world order to some new one whose outlines we still cannot make out. David Graeber has argued that we are in a transitional period in which the global monetary system is transforming, the direction of indebtedness is shifting rapidly, and we don't know where we are heading.[2] The Czech economists Ilona Švihlíková and Miroslav Tejkl write that, as a consequence of the automation of work and of deep technological changes, we are entering a period that has no historical comparison, and thus we lack a template that would indicate how to proceed.[3] Moreover, there is no indication that this turbulent state is coming to its end, and it is quite probable that we still have many decades of social crises and shocks ahead of us. Milan Babic writes in his study on the subject that the "international liberal order" is in a protracted economic and political crisis that began with the financial crisis in 2008,[4] and he uses Gramsci's concept of the crisis as an interregnum in his analysis. Gramsci understood the crisis as a process that has a history: it does not come like a bolt out of the blue, but instead develops within the body of a society. Gramsci terms these deep crises "organic," and when they come about, the political representation is unable to solve the accumulating problems within the framework of the collapsing social order, which then loses its legitimacy. Political actors associated with the given order lose their will to rule, but political actors of another type also don't take over because the kind of order that would enable them to reckon with these difficulties is lacking. Therefore, an interregnum impends. In this Gramscian spirit, Babic and others speak of a "global organic crisis" of capitalism and of human civilization that has reached the stage of a long interregnum. In Gramsci's time, the "morbid symptoms" that appeared in the interregnum included outbreaks of political violence, fascist mass movements, previously unimaginable changes on the political scene, and the sudden breakdown of international agreements. Babic explains that they are morbid because they indicate that the existing social order is dying by virtue of being unable to solve problems that threaten its own survival. I classify the kinds of problems that must be overcome as a condition for the further continuation of the given form of society as "conditional."[5] During an organic social crisis, conditional problems become chronic, and it is essentially impossible for the given form of society to overcome them. In this case, the existing form of society is in the throes of agony, which may last a long time. The interregnum can then be defined as a time in which conditional problems become unsolvable, but the given form of society continues to exist in a certain zombie form. Its problem is that it can't die because nothing on the horizon is coming to replace it.[6]

Let us take note of the difference between Bauman's and Babic's description of the interregnum, in which the global world has found itself. What Bauman has in mind are the changes in the global world since 1989 that have led to a state of uncertainty and the disintegration of the previous conception of territory, state, and national sovereignty. Babic describes the contradictions and crisis tendencies of the "international liberal order" after 2008. Thus, a certain history of the interregnum after 1989 appears before us. Bauman captured the character of the first period of interregnum, in which he insightfully predicted, for example, the phenomenon of mass immigration that would influence political developments in Europe and the United States in the following years. He describes the first period of the interregnum as one of "floating" sovereignty. Babic analyzes the second period of the interregnum (the first appeared to him as "order"). They are distinguished by a "great variety of morbid symptoms," as Gramsci put it. As examples of these symptoms, Babic offers that "illiberal backlashes" in the countries of Central and Eastern Europe that had previously welcomed experimentation with neoliberal politics; the experience in 2017 when a far-right party gained a seat in political representation for the first time since the end of the Second World War; and also Great Britain's exit from the EU, which was provoked by the radical conservative clique around the UK Independence Party—a movement that had previously been considered marginal. Donald Trump's victory in the American presidential election was equally surprising. The spread of radically conservative values and nationalist populism in Italy, France, the Netherlands, and other countries in Europe and elsewhere in the world is also a morbid symptom. Politicians who aimed their rhetoric against the establishment, and who had previously been considered political outsiders, are now acceding to power. In all countries, distrust of neoliberal globalization is growing, and a skeptical attitude toward the power of liberal-democratic representation to deal with the crisis phenomena is spreading.

Bauman's and Babic's application of Gramsci's concept of the interregnum to the present time confirmed my philosophical intuition that our era can be summarized as an interregnum. These thinkers' work prompted me to move beyond mere intuition and develop a theory of the interregnum that expresses the general features of the period that began in 1989. As far as I know, the first to publish the idea that we can understand our period as a Gramscian interregnum was Bauman, and afterward it began to appear in sociological and political science studies on contemporary society.

New Approaches and Concepts

This book offers several new approaches and concepts. In the work, I distinguish between two periods of interregnum: we can date the first one from 1989 to 2008, and the second period from the financial crisis of 2008 to the present time—a distinction that was only found implicitly in Babic and other authors. Another innovation in my approach is that I understand the concept of the interregnum as a conceptual framework for interpreting neoliberalism and postmodernism. I propose the conception of neoliberalism and postmodernism as the dominant ideas of the first period of interregnum. After 1989, these two dominant ideas underwent internal splitting and mutations that manifested significantly in the second period of interregnum, that is, in our present time. This interregnal interpretation of neoliberalism and postmodernism has allowed me to winnow out certain common aspects of these dominant features from the first period of the interregnum. Hopefully, readers will find it revelatory that their main common social feature was the presence of elements that influenced the previous period. I demonstrate that neoliberalism contained "elements of communism," by which I mean it had incorporated various types of egalitarian thought that manifested in diverse social and political forms during the twentieth century. The absorption of the "spirit of 1968" by early neoliberalism was of particular significance. Similarly, postmodernism contained elements of modernism with its avant-garde ambitions and radically emancipatory political horizon. I consider this presence of elements from the previous period to be their common feature, the existence of which can also be explained by proverbial "common sense." Neoliberalism and postmodernism arose in a period in which egalitarian, emancipatory, and modernist ideas still had persuasive power, although their influence was slowly waning. Neoliberalism and postmodernism absorbed them, albeit in an altered form, which is why both neoliberalism and postmodernism were comprehensible and acceptable for society at that time. Neoliberalism, and partially also postmodernism, even gave the impression of being a kind of revolution. For how could neoliberalism have established itself in post-socialist societies in Eastern Europe after 1989 if it hadn't offered a certain egalitarian vision? In Czechoslovakia we were promised that each citizen, with no distinctions, could become a stockholder through coupon privatization and participate in the economy. After 2008 (or, in the case of postmodernism, at the beginning of the new millennium), the weakening of these elements was so evident that they ceased to influence these dominant ideas—and as a result, they began to disintegrate. The thesis about the presence of modernism in postmodernism, or of its "mixed" or "impure" character, in itself, is not a breakthrough: many authors have written about this in one form or another, and their theories will be discussed in the book. The thesis of the egalitarian influence on early neoliberalism is not entirely commonplace, but I believe that I provide sufficient evidence for it. The nature of the transformation of modernism and neoliberalism in the second period of the interregnum (in the past decade) was naturally the subject of many studies in cultural theory and economics. In this book, I propose a thesis on the prosthetic nature of neoliberalism and postmodernism followed by a thesis on their promiscuous nature. As far as I know, these theses have not been formulated in this way anywhere else. They are theses that enable the deduction of general characteristics of the contemporary interregnum, and they are crucial for understanding this work; therefore, it would be apt to express them in summary form now so the reader has a clear orientation through the book's journey.

Summary Thesis on the Origin of the Present Interregnum and Its Circulatory Character

Neoliberalism and postmodernismhave lost their dominant position because the egalitarian and modernist patterns that connected them to the period before the interregnum began have ceased to operate. Neoliberalism and postmodernism developed as dominant forces when they had these supporting models. Neoliberalism and postmodernism display a prosthetic character. The nature of neoliberalism and postmodernism is promiscuous: once the supporting models fell away, neoliberalism and postmodernism began to join together with principles that were originally alien or marginal to them. As a result of their merging in this way, neoliberalism fractures, and mutations of postmodernism appear. (For example, neoliberalism is joined with an imperative to self-sacrifice, and postmodernism merges with conservatism.) The neoliberal model (the market, etc.) and the postmodern model (plurality, etc.) thus lost their dominant position, and their application is co-determined by patterns that were previously alien or marginal to them. Economic, cultural, and political forms are emerging in which no set of patterns holds a dominant position. These forms circulate among mutually alien patterns, and they have a hybrid nature. These circulations (which can be represented as an ellipse) express the character of the present interregnum.

I deduced the prostheticthesis from the "mixed" or "impure" nature of neoliberalism and postmodernism in the first period of the interregnum. In my view, the "mixed" nature of neoliberalism and postmodernism has already been sufficiently documented. I have examined their promiscuous character using a range of phenomena that are appearing in the contemporary economy, culture, and politics. Some of these can be described as Gramscian "morbid symptoms" of the interregnum; for example, the Identitarian movement, radical conservative populism, and the Islamic State. However, other phenomena point in a different direction. Within them can be found tendencies to create new forms of concepts that we know from modernist and radical emancipatory movements of the twentieth century, such as truth, equality, seriousness, reality, concentration, form, and communism. So, besides the morbid symptoms of the interregnum, there also appear symptoms of its possible end.

Another new approach is plotting the general features of the first and second periods of interregnum using geometric models. I present an epicycloid model for the first period of the interregnum and a model of an ellipse for the second period, and I provide the reasons for their introduction in detail in the concluding part of the chapter "Contemporary Culture and Politics as Infinite Circulation." These models are primarily a tool for conceptually grasping the overall character of the interregnum in its first and second periods. They express the basic intention of this book, which was to expand Badiou's concept of intervallic period and Gramsci's notion of interregnum and create an ontology of the present that consists in a recognition of its general characteristics. An interregnum, in its basic meaning that was imprinted by Gramsci, is a blocked transition from one world order to another. Due to this transitive nature of the interregnum, I term this ontology *transitive ontology*.[7]

However, I also give the concept of the interregnum a new layer that Gramsci had only hinted at. He developed his conception of the interregnum on the basis of a Marxist analysis of history, according to which capitalism contains contradictions that cause the system to become unable to provide for the conditions of its own continued existence. Capitalism is not the last socioeconomic system in history, but due to the contradictions contained within it, we can assume a transition to a society that will no longer be organized according to capital's irrational logic. Marx predicted the rise of communism and a society that will freely administer the economy: the main regulator will be equality in the principle of remuneration (in the first phase, there will be "inequality in equality," because some will have greater talent, abilities, and commitment than others, so because they give more to society, they will be rewarded accordingly). The economy will be made up of "free producers" whose income will not be determined by their class position, but will instead be based on what they do for society. This is the historical background against which Gramsci developed his ideas about the interregnum. In broad strokes, he understood the interregnum as a blocked transition from capitalism to communism, although his view did have more political nuances. He also claimed that, although the various political institutions and economic forms connected with capitalism are dying, new ones cannot emerge that will implement the principles of communist society. This historical philosophical background against which Gramsci developed his concept of the interregnum allowed me to connect Gramsci's concept of the interregnum with the conception of the historical interval that we find in Alain Badiou's work. This term refers to the closed sequence of the communist idea and a new sequence of it. Badiou conceives of the communist idea as a fundamentally egalitarian principle that calls into question the reasons for the existence of class inequality and seeks to activate social movements and political forms that embody this principle in given historical circumstances. According to Badiou, we find ourselves in exactly this kind of interval now. However, by contrast with Gramsci, Badiou primarily means a transition from the closed form of communist politics to a form of it that is still unknown. This difference is due to Gramsci having formulated his concept of the interregnum at a time when the sequence of communist ideas that referred to the October Revolution was still playing out. Gramsci formed his conception of the interregnum against the background of this sequence, in which the transition from capitalism to communism appeared to be something realistic that had only been postponed. In this respect, Gramsci's formulation of the interregnum is outdated because it situates the interregnum within the sequence of the communist idea. According to Badiou, we are now in a situation that arose after the conclusion of this sequence. I therefore draw from Badiou's conception of the present period as a historical interval, but I expand it with further characteristics provided by Gramsci's definition of the interregnum. I understand Badiou's notion of the interval as a Gramscian interregnum that is not a sequence within the communist idea because it is sited outside this sequence. Of course, we can claim that our period can also be defined as a period of transition from capitalism to communism, but in this case, what does the word "communism" mean? As Badiou says, today we are struggling to clear away the criminal connotations imputed to the word communism by anticommunists so that the word communism is not only lacking the criminal connotations imputed to it by anticommunists, and also to give it a new semantic potential and so that we can begin to consider the real possibilities of a new conception of communism. We have to adapt Gramsci's statement so it accurately represents today's situation:

> The crisis consists precisely in the fact that the old is dying, and we are unable to imagine that the new can be born; in this interregnum a great variety of morbid symptoms appear.

The present interregnumdiffers from Gramsci's description of the interregnum because, although we are aware that the established institutions and global capitalist system are unable to solve their own existential crisis—that is, that the old order is dying—at the same time, we also believe that nothing new can come—because it seems to us that the idea of communism died along with the system of state socialism. If we adapt Gramsci's statement to correspond with the situation after 1989, Badiou's term semantically corresponds to the historical interval as a period after the communist idea's sequence has ended. This term defines what the present period is following and what will hypothetically follow after it. Badiou's term "interval" refers to the historical succession of individual periods. Gramsci's conception not only refers to this sequence but also provides *character* definitions that we can apply to the present era, which Badiou conceives of as an interval. Badiou himself describes phenomena that appear in the present historical interval so that they correspond to Gramsci's definition. For example, in *The Pornographic Age*, he cites Julian Apostate from Ibsen's piece *Emperor and Galilean*, who balances between the aesthetic inheritance of the Greeks and the Christian revelation, and declares: "The old beauty is no longer beautiful and the new truth is not yet true."[8] Badiou asks, what is the present age, and answers: "it is an age in which the old revolutionary politics is no longer active, and where the new politics is, with difficulty, experimenting with its truth. We are the experimenters of the interval. We are between two worlds, one of which is falling little by little into oblivion, and the other is only fragmentary. It's a matter of passing [passer]."[9]

In this book, I mainly interpret the characteristics of the period after 1989 and examine them through changes in the economy and culture. This is why I have chosen the concept of the interregnum instead of the interval. However, I am changing Gramsci's original concept of the interregnum to make it correspond to the present period that Badiou terms the interval. As far as I know, this is a new, as-yet-unpublished conception that consists in approaching Badiou's notion of the historical interval from the perspective of its character and then understanding it as a Gramscian interregnum.

After acknowledging the influence of this concept of the interregnum, I then propose a new approach to interpreting Badiou's philosophy. When we pose the question of the relationship of Badiou's philosophy to the present interregnum, we can then ask: Is this philosophy part of the cultural logic of the interregnum, or does it transcend this logic? We thus discover the paradoxical position of Badiou's philosophy in relation to the interregnum. On the one hand, Badiou claims that philosophy exists when scientific, political, and artistic truths, and the truth of love are present. However, on the other, he writes that the sequence of political truth has closed. As we will see, he speaks not only of political truth but also of artistic truth and the truth of love. Only the truth of science (mathematics) remains. So how can Badiou's philosophy exist? This is one of the greatest mysteries that interpretations of Badiou have not yet devoted adequate attention to. At the book's conclusion, I claim that Badiou solved this mystery in *The Immanence of Truths*, which was published in French in 2018. From this final part of Badiou's ontological *opus magnum, I deduce a special characteristic of the interregnum as a period in which there are no currently evolving truths (with the exception of scientific truths), but at the same time, it opens up a specific relationship to ideas and infinity.* This concluding section is the most challenging part of the book because here the reader ascends to Badiou's ontology of the infinite, which is based on the difficult mathematical theory of the large cardinals. In Badiou's words, it's similar to ascending the immense Himalayan plateau or a hard-to-reach peak, where we will breathe the heady high-altitude air.[10] Then after this philosophical ascent, the reader may be aware of seeing the panorama of the entire interregnum laid out in front of them.

The question of unity and multiplicity weaves through the book like a red thread. I have chosen these two categories because their presence or absence in neoliberalism and postmodernism, and their transformations, are quite reliable indicators of what tendencies prevail in these domains. Multiplicity appears as an economic principle of the multiplicity of human capital in early neoliberalism, where it was connected with the egalitarian element of the market, which invisibly maintains the correlation between the merits of the individual (i.e., their diligence, industriousness, and creativity) and the rewards the individual receives. In neoliberalism after 2008, this principle of multiplicity comes into opposition to the principle of the unity of the "whole of the healthy economy," which requires self-sacrifice on the part of the neoliberal subject. Similarly, in postmodernism, the radical plurality of the individual in all sorts of variations comes about when there is a radical emancipatory horizon of justice for the individual (Derrida). After this horizon fades away, the radical plurality begins to mutate into a form that serves as a legitimation for conservative or even neofascist movements that aim at restoring the uniqueness and authenticity of cultural communities. The reader will discover the remarkable fact that plurality was conditioned in neoliberalism and postmodernism by the presence of elements that arose from the sequence of the communist idea in the twentieth century.

The question of unity and plurality also winds through the part of the book dedicated to Alain Badiou. The fundamental concepts of his philosophy (the event, truth, and the subject) conceal a new solution to the relationship between unity and plurality, which in my view has no other model in the history of philosophy to date. Badiou created these concepts through discoveries in set theory in the 1960s, which simply had not been available to previous philosophers. The reader will become acquainted with the retrocausal relationship between unity and plurality that acts upon Badiou's conceptions of the event, truth, and the subject.

As for politics in the period of the interregnum, I did not investigate it as an independent domain. I deal with the phenomenon of populist democracy (metapopulism) and the appearance of certain "morbid symptoms" in the subchapter "The domain of politics: the Identitarian movement, the Islamic State, and metapopulism." While writing the book, I also developed a chapter on liberal democracy, which—just like neoliberalism and postmodernism—was one of the dominant ideas of the period after 1989 and took a hybrid political form where egalitarian principles were in operation. These principles—for example, the rule of law, which doesn't take class position into account, or the principle of civic equality—nevertheless weakened as the radical emancipatory ideas bequeathed to us by the twentieth century weakened or were entirely extinguished. The weakening of these egalitarian principles of liberal democracy and the financial crisis of 2008 provoked a populist and even "illiberal" backlash that is changing the character of liberal democracy. However, in the end, I did not include these subjects in the book. This excessive breadth of topics would have obscured the main aim of this book, which is the recognition of general characteristics of the period after 1989 and their structural analysis; or, in other words, the creation of the basics of a transitive ontology of the interregnum. I have decided to investigate the political domain of the interregnum and its transformations in other books.[11]

Organization of the Book

This book consists of anintroduction and two parts that express the historical and logical sequence of the phenomena investigated. The Introduction deals with the prehistory of the interregnum, the first part focuses on the present interregnum, and the second part interprets Badiou's philosophy as a possible exit (exodus) from the interregnum. The Introduction is more extensive than is typical because it describes the extinction of the communist idea, including knotty issues such as Stalinism. It also covers the events of May 1968 in France, the Chinese Cultural Revolution, the Prague Spring, and the following two decades, during which the impossibility of continuing in the communist sequence of the twentieth century became evident because no new solutions for its internal contradictions appeared. I conceive of this period as the interregnum because it was in the space of the extinguishing elements of this sequence that neoliberalism and postmodernism took shape as the future dominant features of the first period of the interregnum.

In Part One, titled "The Eccentric Interregnum," I address the two periods of the interregnum. In the first section of this part, I examine the presence of egalitarian elements in neoliberalism and the egalitarian and modernist elements in postmodernism, which these domains had absorbed in the period of their formation in the two decades after 1968. I carry out a kind of anamnesis of their genesis (Adorno), and therefore mainly analyze their early phase, which dates back to before 1989. Part One confines its analysis to the years 1989–2000/2008. At that time, both neoliberalism and postmodernism were present in the forms they took on during the previous period, and they were the dominant ideas of this first period of the interregnum (I provide the year 2000 because it is the customary date for the end of postmodernism). The second section of Part One focuses on the second period of the interregnum, which has endured until the present time. In it, I examine the splitting of neoliberalism and the mutations of postmodernism, which have been caused by their prosthetic and promiscuous character. This part contains the book's main theoretical advances that were mentioned above. Here, one can read about the contemporary discussions of neoliberalism and postmodernism and also about their promiscuous unions. In the case of postmodernism, I present significant examples of this promiscuity (the Identitarian movement and the Islamic State). At the end of this part, I propose to distinguish the diverse formations within the contemporary interregnum according to their tendencies toward being obscure (religious-fundamentalist tendencies), reactive (negation of the traces of past events), and pre-evental (a tendency toward the origin of a new event). I call the whole Part One the "Eccentric Interregnum" because neither the neoliberal pattern nor the postmodern one in either the first or the second period have an uninterrupted central position. They are exposed to the influences of patterns in an eccentric position (egalitarian principles or modernism in the first, "epicyclical" period) or they are no longer dominant and are in equilibrium with patterns of all kinds of other origins (conservative, populist, religious, etc. in the second, "elliptical" period). I conclude Part One with a summary, but I deliberately leave the end of this part without a summarizing closure in order to express that its content has not been closed, because it relates to our present and to various tendencies that are continuing to develop.

In Part Two of the book, in connection to the pre-evental tendencies, I focus on Badiou's philosophy in relation to the interregnum. I present it on the basis of two axes of interpretation: the first interpretive axis is the question of how Badiou's philosophy is even possible in the interregnum; that is, in a situation after the closure of truths. The second axis concerns the relationship of unity and plurality in his fundamental concepts of the event, truth, and the subject. It transpires that Badiou's philosophy can be conceived as a second version of transitive ontology. The first version is the transitive ontology that was elaborated upon in Part One of the book. This kind comprises the recognition of the general characteristics of the interregnum as a period of transition. Badiou's version of transitive ontology creates the intellectual conditions for the renewal of truth procedures in politics, art, and love, which herald the arrival of a new era of truths that will close the period of the interregnum. *Transitive ontology* can be read as a discipline that deals with *periods* of transition, which have appeared in human history since the Neolithic Revolution through the "dark centuries" between antiquity and the Middle Ages, the transition from the Middle Ages to the modern era, all the way to the present time.

The book ends with the statement that the interregnum opens up a specific relationship to ideas that evokes a longing for the discovery of truths. Since it began with Badiou's concept of the idea serving as a reference point in today's world, the end of the book thus evokes a new understanding of this starting point.

Introduction

The Liberating Power of Generalization and the Prehistory of the Interregnum

Capital and the Idea as Landmarks (Jameson and Badiou)

Jameson's famous formulation, which claimed that we are in a historical period in which people have forgotten to think historically, remained valid for fifty years after the rise of the postmodernism to which this formulation specifically refers. We are still in a period in which the diagnosis of the period appears as an enterprise doomed to fail because we are unsure of whether anything as general as a "period," Zeitgeist, "system," or "present situation" even exists.[1] According to Jameson, this apparent impossibility is mainly caused by a weakening and disappearance of the general or universalizing concepts that are the condition of such a diagnosis. Without an idea of the meaning of generalizing terms such as history or era, the problem of the diagnosis of the period itself appears as pointless. Jameson humorously remarks that the waning of our sense of history, and more particularly our resistance to universalizing concepts, is a function of the universalization of capitalism.[2] Different socioeconomic enclaves that had survived until now have disappeared from capitalism as capitalism has become truly ubiquitous and global. This is precisely the time when the idea of the system as a whole becomes very difficult and almost impossible. Universalizing concepts disintegrate when a given system has become universalized to the point that it swallows up the last truly different worlds that enabled the creation of ideas of something other than itself. Renewing at least the hypothesis that another world besides capitalism is possible ought to be the condition under which reviving universalizing concepts can take place. It follows from Jameson's ideas that universalizing concepts and a diagnosis of the period will be considered more necessary the more the search for the possibility of another world appears, and the more the limits of the system become apparent. From this perspective, the introduction of universalizing concepts is a certain form of disagreement with a system in which resistance to them became a manifestation of its universalism.

Jameson writes that capitalism has never had such a wide field of activity at any time in history as it has since the 1980s. All the forces it summoned against itself in the past that could have threatened it—such as workers' movements and revolts or mass-based socialist parties—are disoriented and essentially neutralized. In Jameson's view, this system is undergoing a transformation on a global scale and we are in a transitional period between two stages of capitalism. This critical culture theorist characterizes postmodernism as transitional period, and he believes that the global transformation of the system will give rise to a new international proletariat that will take forms we cannot yet imagine.[3]

In this time of transition, there is a deep disorientation that Jameson compares to a city that has no landmarks that would allow us to form an idea of where we are. He claims that a new space has emerged in which the distance toward a given place that used to be indicated by landmarks, as well as our awareness of the overall structure of the space, has been suppressed. Moreover, the postmodern body is overwhelmed by its perception of immediacy since mediating instances have been removed. Individuals find themselves in a multidimensional space of radically discontinuous realities, in which the privacy of individual life intersects with the decentering of global capitalism, which transcends the human imagination. As Jameson says, lived experience is fragmented, decentered, and dispersed, and it has a schizophrenic nature.[4] This lived experience gives rise to the belief that even searching for orientation makes no sense. Jameson shows the paradoxical character of the representation of the social system in the transitional postmodern period. The very form of representation—which corresponded to the previous stage of capitalism, in which the imperial powers defined the visible boundaries of their spheres of influence—has disintegrated. In a time when a new system of globalized capital is just taking shape, it is impossible in principle to capture this process through an established mode of representation because it would not correspond to the situation of transition that we find ourselves in. Jameson proposes to develop a cognitive mapping that approaches the global social reality as though it were a city in which we link immediate individual experience with the idea that the city forms a certain whole that cannot presently be represented. The failure of the previous mode of representation thus offers a starting point for the dialectical recognition of the infinite complexity of the new global space: we connect our fragmented experiences of it with generalizing concepts as a formal framework of the experiencing. According to Jameson, these generalizations crystallize, thanks to the fact that even in the period of transition, a certain unifying and totalizing power—the "nonhuman" logic of capital—is operating.[5] However, discontinuity and fragmentation of space are not the only aspects that we might use to characterize the period of transition. In parallel with the process of fragmentation, a certain unification and homogenization are proceeding, which are the uncontrollable effects of capital as a unified expansive pattern. A new type of dialectic between fragmentation and homogenization appears, whose contours were sketched by Jameson with the awareness that in the period of transition, this dialectic lacks a clear outline. For Jameson, the guidepost for a cognitive mapping of our position in the global system in the period of transition is capital itself, as an anonymous force that creates a generalizing framework into which we insert a seemingly entirely unrepresentable variety of fragments, discontinuities, and partial horizons. According to Jameson, in the time of the transition, we should orient ourselves according to the coordinates created by global capital.

However, besides global capital, there is another landmark that of course is only present in Jameson's cognitive mapping as an indefinite circumstance that does not become involved in creating the orientation coordinates: the effect of the hypothesis or the idea of communism, which Alain Badiou writes about. In the first approximation, Badiou defines it generally as a regulating idea of equality or as an egalitarian maximum that has the nature of a hypothesis with two corresponding meanings. Expressed negatively, it casts doubt on the "inevitability" of monstrous inequalities and the "necessity" of the subordinate position of the people who work for the ruling class; however, in its positive sense, it is a set of ideas that show that another form of social organization can be realized. According to Badiou, this set forms the horizon of every initiative that splits from the established thoughts, ideas, and opinions, and it "composes a fragment of a politics of emancipation."[6] The communist idea expresses the possibility of a society whose social organization is not determined by class positions but is given shape by a fundamental equality among people. This is not an equality of everyone in everything, as the cheap anticommunist argument goes, but the application of the principle of equality among people in the social and power order of society. This principle establishes equal conditions for developing the abilities and human dimensions of each individual and shapes a society that is aware that its economic, scientific, and cultural development depends on the qualities of each of its members, so it supports each person's advancement. Equality in the form of civic equality is enshrined in all democratic constitutions, which generally contain the principle of their extension into further spheres in the form of social and cultural rights. From this perspective, communism is supposed to be the fulfillment of the egalitarian spirit of democratic constitutions. As we will see in the beginning of the section dedicated to contemporary culture, in the subchapter "Metamodernism, remodernism, altermodernism . . . the multiple names of contemporary culture," I will show that Badiou is not the only philosopher who supplies the "communist idea" with a positive meaning today. Besides him, other thinkers who are coming from different starting points are also writing about this idea in a positive spirit, including Slavoj Žižek, Gianni Vattimo, Michael Hardt, Antonio Negri, Jacques Rancière, Jodi Dean, Bruno Bosteels, Alberto Toscano, and Frank Ruda.

The idea of communism had many different incarnations in the nineteenth and twentieth centuries, from radical democratic currents in the period of the French Revolution to the Paris Commune, the Russian Revolution, 1968, and up to the Polish Solidarity movement. When Jameson writes that postmodernism arrived as a period of transition at the time when all the forces that threatened capitalism disappeared, he indirectly proves that the period of transition appeared when the idea of communism had ceased to operate as a historical factor. The forces of resistance against capitalism were various expressions of the idea that it is possible to create a society founded on the principle of equality. Badiou focuses on the social embodiment of this idea in the nineteenth and especially in the twentieth century with the perspective that one of its historical sequences has ended and the next has not yet begun. Badiou thus introduces the idea of communism as a point of reference, which Jameson does not thematize as a separate issue and understands only as one of the preconditions for the existence of historical movements that have stood in opposition to capitalism. However, Jameson and Badiou do not contradict each other because both of them put the beginning of the period of transition into the context of the retreat or demise of radical emancipatory movements.

Why Prefer the Idea of Communism over Liberalism?

Answers to Possible Objections

Badiou takes a non-obvious step by understanding modern political history in relation to the idea of communism and dividing it into periods in which the idea of communism had political and social incarnations, and a period of an "interval" in which this idea appeared impracticable and politics obeyed the imperatives of capital and legitimized social class inequality as an unchangeable fact. Badiou's periodization certainly invites a number of questions and could even seem dogmatic to some. We can raise the objection that Badiou does not attribute any special significance to the liberally ordered society that was the dominant political form of the last two centuries. He considers politics related to the idea of communism to be an exception that appears in an established political and economic system. Why, then, does the liberal period of modern history represent a mere interval between these exceptions? If we understand this interval as a Gramscian interregnum, it ought to be a period between two relatively stabilized political-economic systems. Wasn't the liberal social order stable? And if so, why consider it an interregnum? In addition, it can be argued that the immediate goal of revolutionary politics tied to the idea of communism was not to establish a different stable system, but to change social relations and the power structure so that the starting conditions were formed for the transition to a new social system called communism. The October Revolution can be understood as at best creating the starting conditions for long-term processes out of which a generally freer and more humane society than the class society could arise. Even in the official documents of the socialist dictatorships, it was stated that the postrevolutionary society was on a long and difficult path toward communism. As will be discussed later, according to Badiou, a solution to the question of state structure in relationship to the idea of communism was not found in the twentieth century. The state structure was supposed to protect the results of the revolution, but at the same time, it also blocked the transition to communism. The entire process got stuck somewhere in the early stages and instead of a transition to a more humane type of society, a metastasis took place, and state terror, bureaucratization, and the new privileged classes (the nomenklatura) appeared.

Before addressing these objections, we need to answer the question of exactly what the decision to prioritize liberal values is based on, and to create a periodization in which, instead, the period of the social influence of the communist idea is considered to be an interval between two periods of "freedom and democracy." It is generally claimed that socialist dictatorships were "totalitarian" closed societies that were inhumane or even criminal, and they were distinguished by the violent suppression of the rights and freedoms of the great majority of society. As the case of the historian Michal Pullmann in 2020 shows, the media presentation of scholarly studies and arguments that cast doubt on this official picture of the past regime are interpreted as an insult to the regime's victims. This issue is highly politicized today and arouses a great deal of emotion, and it is therefore difficult for the history of science and philosophy to do their work and acquaint the public with the fact that this official interpretation is not the only possible one. In socialist dictatorships, the tension between violent practice and the humanist social goal never ceased to exist. This tension was aptly expressed by Maurice Merleau-Ponty in the book *Humanism and Terror*, where he writes that "neither Bukharin nor Trotsky nor Stalin regarded Terror as intrinsically valuable. Each one imagined that he was using it to realize a genuinely human history which had not yet started but which provides the justification for revolutionary violence."[7] As Merleau-Ponty proves, the difference between the Western democracies and the socialist regimes did not lie in the problem of violence, but in the question of its meaning. According to this philosopher, the one-sided advocates of Western democracy hush it up when Western democracies engage in military interventions, which are also a form of violence, and they downplay the inhumane aspects of capitalist society. They then compare the idealized image of Western democracies with the image of the socialist countries, where they emphasize the violent practices. Thus, according to Merleau-Ponty, the violence and numbers of victims themselves are not a sufficient criterion for evaluating the legitimacy of capitalist democracies and socialist regimes, because both of these systems invoke humanist principles when using violence.[8] What follows from counting 65 to 93 million "victims of communism" as the authors of the *Black Book of Communism* have done, or 165 million victims of capitalism in the twentieth century as was done by the authors of the *Black Book of Capitalism*?[9] If both capitalist democracies and socialist dictatorships legitimized themselves using humanist principles, Merleau-Ponty's argument demonstrates that, in the period of the existence of the socialist countries, there was no *purely logical* reason to prefer one system over the other. Preferences are often developed from the kind of image one adopts to represent these systems. As we will see below, Badiou concluded that at the end of the 1970s, the sequence of the communist idea of the twentieth century had closed, because no attempt at changing the socialist systems in such a way that processes leading to communism as the actualization of egalitarian principles had taken place. Thus, these systems lost their legitimacy. In the book, I express essentially the same position as Badiou, but even so, I am aware that even then it was possible to argue, as the Czech philosopher Egon Bondy had in *Rambling Monologue* [Neuspořádaná samomluva], that the civilizational regression in the period of socialism, which was ruled by "the new ruling class," is analogous to the civilizational regression that took place in early feudalism. The early feudal society doubtlessly looks like economic (and other kinds of) barbarism and a backsliding, and according to Bondy, it took many centuries until feudalism developed to a level where it was more civilizationally progressive than a system of slavery. It may also take centuries before the socialist system shows its inner potential to reach a higher civilizational level than capitalism.[10]

The only compelling reason to favor liberal-democratic capitalism was formulated by Francis Fukuyama: he argues that it's a fait accompli. The collapse of the socialist bloc means that this system has not *actually* worked. It then follows that the only proven system that is legitimized by humanist principles is liberal-democratic capitalism.[11] If, on the contrary, socialism had (hypothetically) managed to transition into a humane and free form of society with well-rounded development, but liberal-democratic capitalism had collapsed, according to Fukuyama's logic it would mean that socialism had proven itself successful and its victory would mark the end of political history. The historian Eric Hobsbawm shocked viewers in an interview with Michael Ignatieff on the BBC in 1994 when he stated, "the death of millions of Soviet citizens under Stalin would have been worth it if the result was a true communist society."[12] If we accept Fukuyama's logic, this shocking statement is justified. In the history of capitalist countries, there have been millions of deaths due to colonialism, slavery, violence committed against native populations, and so on. For example, according to a recently published study, the famine in Bengal in 1943, which claimed 3 million lives, is the responsibility of Winston Churchill, who had no regard for the local population and did nothing to cease the export of foodstuffs to Great Britain.[13] However, these victims are viewed differently than the victims of Stalinism, even though from the perspective of human rights, there is no difference between one politician who causes the death of a Ukrainian (such as during the famine in Ukraine under Stalin) and another politician's decision that causes the death of a Bengali. The different assessment of these victims arises out of the fact that liberal-democratic capitalism emerged victorious. The common argument goes that although capitalism had many victims, it's allegedly thanks to capitalism that today the great majority of society enjoys a high living standard. If the promise of politicians (as voiced by M. Thatcher, for example) that the defeat of socialist ideas and the strengthening of capitalism will lead to affluence had been fulfilled, the sacrifices of capitalism would have been worth it. Millions of victims of capitalism are thus assigned a value that inheres in their having enabled today's affluence and having contributed to the overall development of civilization. In this way, "democratic" politicians, economists, and part of the public retroactively justify the violence of colonial and other capitalist practices with their countless victims. This justification for past crimes was common until recently, and hardly shocked anyone, even though it justified millions of dead in an intellectually similar manner as Hobsbawm's shocking statement.

After 1989, the view spread that "communism" and "Nazism" represented the same "totalitarian evil" and there was no fundamental difference between them. However, this view is based on a similar ideological operation as the one described by Merleau-Ponty: covering up the sides of the regime being evaluated that don't fit the image being constructed of it. We can only identify Nazism and communism if we cover up the fact that "communist regimes" enshrined the principle of civic and human rights in their constitutions. The Soviet constitution from 1936 establishes the right to private ownership (Article 10), the independence of courts from state power (Article 112), the right to education, free study, and instruction in native languages (118), the equality of men and women in all spheres of social life (Article 122), the legal equality of all citizens regardless of their ethnicity or race (Article 123), freedom of conscience (Article 124), freedom of speech, the press, and assembly (Article 125), and the inviolability of the person and the household (Article 127). Let's compare these provisions with the Nazi "Nuremberg Laws" from 1935—that is, from the same period as the Soviet constitution. They stipulate that marriages between Jews and German nationals are forbidden and that such marriages are invalid (Law for the Protection of German Blood and German Honor). Another provision is that only a subject of the state who has German or related blood can be a citizen of the Reich, and they are the sole bearers of full political rights (Reich Citizenship Law). After the Second World War, the Soviet Union, along with Czechoslovakia and other allied countries, took part in the preparation of the *Universal Declaration of Human Rights*. As Samuel Moyn shows, this activity was understood to be consistent with the principles contained in the Soviet constitution. When the negotiations among the Great Powers were taking place, there was a controversy over whether collective and social rights were going to be enshrined in the *Declaration* next to individual rights. The Soviet side succeeded in negotiating the incorporation of social rights; however, in the end, they did not sign the document, mainly because the colonial powers refused to include a right to national self-determination in the *Declaration*, which the Soviet Union had insisted on including in the UN Charter in 1945.[14] It is absurd to imagine Nazi Germany taking part in the creation of the *Universal Declaration of Human Rights* because Nazi laws were in stark contrast to it. Equally absurd is the idea that a parallel to Charter 77 could have been created in Nazi Germany. To wit: Nazi Germany complied with its inhuman laws, while Czechoslovakia, the Soviet Union, and other socialist countries did not comply with their humane ones. Charter 77 could only be created because the socialist constitution at that time guaranteed civil and human rights, and their observance was confirmed by Czechoslovak officials at the Conference on Security and Cooperation in Europe that had taken place in Helsinki in 1975. Charter 77 invoked the country's constitution and the institutions and human rights commitments made in Helsinki, which the regime was not upholding. A human rights and civic initiative such as Charter 77 would have been inconceivable in Nazi Germany. Indeed, the very existence of Charter 77 testifies to the fundamental difference between Nazism and communism, which must be taken into account if we are to understand Czechoslovak and world history in their complexity. Charter 77 proves that, in socialist dictatorships, a tension was present between the humanistic ideal of a communist society and the violent or bureaucratic social practice that legitimized itself with these ideals.

Now let us turn to objections that have been raised. In connection with the concept of the interregnum that I develop in this book, the main question is why I favor Badiou's perspective on the communist idea over the perspective of liberal values, even though there were liberally ordered systems in periods of interregnum or in Badiou's interval. As stated in the preface, liberal-democratic capitalism can be considered a stable system whose gradual disintegration we now perceive as a threat to our security. Why, then, do I conceive of liberal-democratic capitalism as a transitional system while understanding various unsuccessful attempts at creating an egalitarian human society as historically authoritative? Am I not refusing to acknowledge the historical significance of the liberal organization of Western society, which has been the dominant social form for the past two hundred years? Aren't I trivializing liberalism, which also represents an autonomous history-forming idea? How can I then explain that I understand liberalism's period of political dominance as a transitional interval between two attempts at the social realization of the idea of communism?

I can answer these objections by saying that liberalism, as well as conservatism and socialism, can be conceived in two manners: on the one hand, as sets of ideals, concepts, and ideas that appear in various renditions in liberal, conservative, and socialist theories, and on the other as various types of political behavior that set the goal of actualizing the corresponding ideals, concepts, and ideas in the given socioeconomic reality. If in liberalism, conservatism, and socialism, we only see three sets of ideals, concepts, and ideas, we will proceed to explain the reasons why we prefer one of these trends. In the final instance, our decision is axiomatic in nature. Why did we decide to accept the freedom of the individual as the authoritative ideal we use to judge other ideals? In principle, there is no other answer than that we just decided to do it because we decided to. Our decision cannot be further substantiated. Although we can prove that freedom is part of human nature, human nature also has many other aspects, including digestion, and we have decided for the ideal of freedom, and not for ideal digestion. At this level, it is impossible to decide based on reasons of principle whether a given direction is "in itself" more worthy than the other directions, because this decision is again axiomatic, and therefore ultimately only justifiable through the act of making a decision itself. However, axiomatic choice is less common than the consensual adoption of a certain ideal or principle that is evoked by a consensus of the opinions in one's immediate surroundings, or in the community or society. One accepts the ideal of freedom because the others accept it. If we remain at the level of ideals and principles, I can present the decision to favor the principle of equality, which is the authoritative principle of socialism and communism, as merely an axiomatic decision that has the same status as a decision to favor the liberal principle of freedom or to favor the conservative "traditional values," that are supposed to preserve the communality of the family and community.

However, the system of axiomatic choices changes when we connect the theoretical level with the question of the real actualization of the ideals of liberalism, conservatism, and socialism. The true realization of a certain ideal is something entirely different than a discussion of its normative claims, which takes place at a theoretical level. Even if we agree in a rational discussion that a certain ideal is normatively the most persuasive, this ideal will not yet have been applied in social practice. This finding seems trivial, but for theorists who are operating only at the first level, it always takes a certain amount of time before they realize its seriousness. The question is then why, in the social practice of liberal democracy, the ideals whose normative obligatory force is not put into practice among, in Kantian terms, the "enlightened public"? There is a consensus today among the enlightened public and even among representatives of international institutions that we are facing at the very least two crucial civilizational problems: an extreme growth in social inequality and an ongoing ecological crisis. So why does this recognized normative commitment generally remain only at a rhetorical level? The problem of extreme inequality is explained by, for instance, Thomas Piketty in his book *Capital in the Twenty-First Century*, and the ecological problem by, for instance, Naomi Klein in her book *This Changes Everything: Capitalism vs the Climate*, in which these authors lay out convincing arguments that liberal democracy is so intertwined with the capitalist economic system that it is essentially impossible to push through even the kinds of decisions that would lead to the preservation of the status quo if these decisions are in conflict with the immediate interests of the financial oligarchy.[15]

These and many other studies indicate that the present socioeconomic system is in a state of Gramscian organic crisis, in which the individual crisis phenomena and contradictions (economic, ecological, social, cultural, and mental) are tied into one knot that cannot be picked apart without system-wide change.[16] I am relying here on analyses that have long been understood by the broader public as manifestations of a kind of Marxist negativism that underrates capitalism's capacity for self-regeneration. Today, however, authors who do not have a background in systematic analysis inspired by Marxist critique are also describing the concurrence of crisis tendencies, such as the Czech climatologist Václav Cílek, who speaks of a composite crisis.[17] During the Covid-19 pandemic, this state manifested in the many problems that affected health care systems and had specific impacts at the level of populations' physical existence, so perhaps the Covid-19 pandemic may represent a turning point in the understanding of the present socioeconomic system.[18] A broad consensus is being formed on the need to change global capitalism not only among critical theorists and socialists but also among liberals, conservatives, various social movements, and even representatives of international institutions. For example, Klaus Schwab, the executive chairman of the World Economic Forum (WEF), speaks of a need to "redefine" global capitalism in a way that does not only take financial capital into account but also focuses on various other types of capital. If this does not happen, he said we can expect a "violent" change of the entire economic system.[19]

This emerging consensus is a clear confirmation of the theories that point to the real possibility or even the necessity of systemic change, in whatever way we understand it. In contemporary capitalism, the individual crisis phenomena and contradictions have interlinked, and an organic or composite crisis has emerged. However, these contradictions and crisis tendencies have taken various forms throughout the history of capitalism. Today's overall crisis consists in their intensification and interlinkage rather than in their appearance as a previously unknown phenomenon. Engels, for example, has already written that by seeking immediate profit, capitalism destroys natural conditions and, as a result, forfeits this profit in the future. Modern capitalism has developed in the last two centuries, which brought unprecedented productive capacity and social wealth into the period, but at the same time, it also created a structure of the relations between power and economics that maintains and deepens social inequality and gives rise to crises and international conflicts. As we know from the history of the twentieth century, the economic crisis of the 1930s enabled the rise of

Nazism in Germany and indirectly led to the outbreak of the Second World War. The liberal order of Western society was never sufficiently protected from these results of the crisis of capitalism, and it is no coincidence that conservative populism began to spread after the 2008 financial crisis. In pursuing its ideals and principles such as individual freedoms, liberalism is always confronted with these consequences of capitalism, which led to a deadly threat from the Nazi and fascist dictatorships in the 1930s. The last two hundred years have been full of upheavals, domestic conflicts within states, and wars, and it can hardly be characterized as a period of stability. The liberal order gained stability only after the Second World War, in a period when most of the world was divided into the Western and Eastern Blocs.

The dominant form of capital has also changed over the course of modern history. For example, in the period of the postwar welfare state, "productive capital" focused on investments predominated, while in the neoliberal economy, financial capital is dominant. This development has led to the state of affairs in today's socioeconomic system where fictitious capital, which grows when debts are increased, is the dominant type. This capital is not based on the production of economic value, which, to put it in simplified terms, is the creation of useful things (including infrastructure, science, and technology), but rather produces the "anti-value" of debt.[20] Therefore, it is entirely legitimate to consider other socioeconomic principles than capital, whose development has reached the stage of fictitious capital. In today's discussions, there is sometimes talk of the "postcapitalist society," but this term is devoid of content and does not indicate the character of the possible future society. Despite all the negative associations, Badiou and many of the above-mentioned theorists use the concept of communism, which suggests that the dominant socioeconomic principle should be that which is "communist": that is, this principle will have the form of social sharing, such as "commonly owned goods" (commons) according to the proposal by Hardt and Negri. The principle of equality thus acquires a more specific socioeconomic form, which needs to be further discussed.[21]

The word "communism," especially in countries of the former Eastern Bloc, functions in the public space as a synonym for the totalitarian "evil empire," and a *reductio ad Gulag* is performed in which the internal tensions and legitimation strategies are translated into the perspective of its victims. As I mentioned above, the previous regime did not consider itself to be communist, and it officially understood communism to be a distant goal which society faced difficulties in moving toward. However, the mission of philosophy is to call the meaning of concepts back to memory, even when these concepts are perceived as "totalitarian." This was already done by Erich Fromm, who explained in the United States in the 1960s that "communism" means a society that is the realization of freedom and political and economic democracy.[22] According to Fromm and Marx, the goal of communism is the well-rounded development of the personality of each individual, which is a condition for the development of the entire society. Therefore, I can argue that this society is to create the preconditions for the actualization of the ideas of humanism, including the liberal principles of individual freedom and even the conservative effort to preserve and develop a sense of communality. The idea of communism does not contradict any principles of modern liberalism or conservatism, but means the creation of the kinds of socioeconomic conditions that enable their real social fulfillment. The concept of "communism" has a meaning diametrically opposite to the one generally attributed to it in the contemporary public space. The word communism has a bad ring to it in today's society, but the same was also true for the concept of democracy, which in the nineteenth century and sometimes even later evoked negative reactions; conservative elites were hostile to democracy, which was seen as tantamount to communism. For instance, in the British Isles, the word "democracy" retained a pejorative meaning until the end of the nineteenth century.[23] Just as the perception of the word democracy has undergone fundamental change, the public perception of the concept of communism can change as well.

To the objection that by favoring the idea of communism I trivialize the historical significance of liberalism, I answer that I conceive of this idea in such a way that it expresses a hypothetical socioeconomic order of a society that arises out of the previous developments of modern liberalism. This idea concerns the change in socioeconomic conditions that are in such a state today that, due to an organic or composite systemic crisis, there is a risk that liberalism will be pushed aside by radical conservatism, similarly to how it was marginalized by fascism and Nazism in the 1930s. Modern liberalism has created concepts that certainly had the power to influence history in the nineteenth and twentieth centuries, but if we are reacting to the present—and not the past state of affairs—it is justified to believe that liberalism has lost this power as a result of the current organic crisis of the socioeconomic system. What does the principle of individual freedom mean in the face of the environmental crisis? Or what does the right to sovereignty over one's own body mean in an age when the genes that are part of our bodies are regulated by the private property rights of corporations that have patented them? A change in the nature of ownership is logically a precondition for these liberal principles to be applied without these contradictions. The idea of communism is the idea of a society that builds on the previous development of these principles and creates the conditions for their renaissance. Working in this direction with the hypothesis of an alternative society is therefore an expression of ordinary common sense. It is somewhat unreasonable to believe that a house that is falling apart due to cracks in the walls will remain standing immobile and will continue to provide safe shelter.

I understand Badiou's idea of communism and the periodization of modern history related to it, which gives rise to his theory of the interregnum, not only in terms of the normative egalitarian principle, which belongs to the first "theoretical" level in our scheme, but also from the perspective of the second level, which in our case means from the perspective of the present organic or composite crisis of the socioeconomic system. In modern history, it was during the periods when political and social processes were underway that the idea of communism took on concrete, real forms—so these times have special significance. In other words, in these periods, the hypothesis of an egalitarian society acted as a history-making force and in one way or another, changed the real form of the world. The idea of communism, which today gives the impression of not being possible to actually realize, then seemed impossible not to realize. At the same time, traps and blind alleys appeared, which caused the cessation and later the extinction of the developing alternative to the capitalist system. I look at these periods from the point of view of the main question of our time, which is whether and how a socioeconomic system that overcomes the organic crisis that is endemic to the present interregnum can be created. The question can be understood as follows: Is it really possible for a society to emerge whose outlines express the idea of communism? My starting point is the present state of the world, and therefore I have decided to adopt Badiou's periodization of modern history.

The Magic of Periodization and Three Conceptual Cities

Badiou and Jameson are among the few contemporary thinkers who deal with historical periodization and define the present as a specific *historical* period. Badiou creates his historical periodization with the awareness that the idea of history itself is merely a conceptual analytical framework that lacks ontological justification. History as an objectively given set of events, phenomena, and connections, does not exist because there are only unique worlds with their "presences," and they draw their strength from the development of those elements of the past that have the proper prerequisites.[24] Badiou's historical periodization has not yet been given due attention from interpreters or critics who have thus far interpreted his conception as practically ahistorical ideas that are composed without reference to specific historical situations. As Bruno Bosteels points out, Badiou shows a sense of historical periodization that often eludes his readers.[25] However, I consider Badiou's sense of periodization and historical grasp of the present time to be the key to his entire oeuvre. In the book, I prove that Badiou's work has arisen as an answer to the situation that came about after the conclusion of the historical sequence marked between 1917 and 1978, with its extinction taking place in the 1980s.

Badiou distinguishes between two sequences of the communist idea in his historical periodization. The first sequence begins with the French Revolution and ends with the Paris Commune, and thus roughly spans the years 1792–1871. The main question in this sequence was whether the communist hypothesis would gain political significance and in what form it should be realized in society. It appeared in various political currents that combined mass people's movements with the theme of seizing power. The highest form of this combination was embodied by the Paris Commune, where the people's movement, with its working-class leadership, accessed immediate political power for a short time. According to Badiou, the second sequence lasted from the Russian Revolution in 1917 until the second half of the 1970s. It concludes in 1976, when the Cultural Revolution was called off in China, and in 1978, after the decade of political experiments that were catalyzed by the revolutionary events of 1968 in France and elsewhere had ended. In this sequence, the topic of the real possibility of communism was no longer discussed. The main question was how to gain victory and organize a new state in such a way as to defend it against enemies and maintain the results of the revolution.[26] There was a period of almost forty years between the two periods in which the "enemy" gained the upper hand, and the hypothesis of communism appeared to be uncertain and unrealizable—Badiou terms this period the interval phase. It reappeared in the second half of the 1970s and continues to this day,[27] and it conceives of communism as an unrealizable utopia at best and a dangerous or even criminal idea at worst. As Badiou says, our problem is that we cannot return to the mass workers' movements of the nineteenth century (the first sequence) or to a communist party of the twentieth century; that is, to the two already familiar materializations of the communist idea. We therefore face an extremely difficult and extraordinarily complicated task, which is finding a different modality for the communist idea that will bring it to new life. Until then, the politics of emancipation will lack orientation and will proceed experimentally, hesitatingly, and chaotically.[28] Badiou therefore argues that the primary task in the present interval phase is the same as that of the revolutionaries of the nineteenth century. The communist hypothesis no longer has social influence, and our goal is to make it exist at all.

In the book *The Pornographic Age*, Badiou expresses himself in a manner reminiscent of Gramsci's definition of the interregnum. As we saw above, Badiou writes that the old politics of emancipation is no longer active and the new one is having difficulties experimenting with its truths. We are between two worlds: one is falling into oblivion and the other is fragmentary. The old truths no longer hold valid, and "the new truth is not yet true . . . It's a matter of passing [passer]."[29] Badiou speaks of emancipatory thinkers and politicians as experimenters of the interval, describing them as "smugglers" who are bringing fragments from the past world into the present situation, in which we create a "politics without fetishes" from these fragments.[30]

In his sequences, Badiou's communist idea thus provides an orientation point for the creation of a theory of the present interregnum, which appears as a confusing and inconsistent collection of political negotiations, trade balances, surveys, information, social and individual experiences, and artistic expressions. Badiou's landmark allows us to pass through this confusing flood of phenomena and maintain a distance from it, which is necessary for this smuggling activity. From the smuggled fragments, a new horizon is crystallizing, from which we measure the catastrophic horizon of this era. Jameson's cognitive mapping focuses on creating coordinates that enable the determination of the social place where we find ourselves. Its goal is to aid individuals in realizing their position in global capitalism with its postmodern culture, in which these coordinates appear to be impossible. Cognitive mapping provides some guidance for forming "class consciousness" in the postmodern transition period. However, it does not provide indicators we can use for moving through this alienated city that symbolizes the contemporary world. Perhaps, thanks to cognitive mapping, we may be able to determine our position, but what are we going to do next? Jameson does not address the question of which direction to head in, and why we should even be heading anywhere. If we stick with Jameson's metaphor of the city, Badiou conceives of his place in this city as the position of a smuggler who moves through the city in order to build a new city from smuggled fragments. As soon as he succeeds in founding the new city, a point appears on the horizon that all the inhabitants can use to orient themselves. Jameson is concerned with the contemporary world as an alienated city, but he actually has one city in mind.

Badiou distinguishes among three cities: the defunct city which embodies the work of the previous emancipatory politics, then the city of the present world which we are walking through like smugglers, and the city that should arise out of the fragments rescued from the first city. These three cities appear at the time when we begin to work with Badiou's periodization related to the idea of communism.

We can compare the present world not only to a city but also to a landscape: Dante's thick, impassable forest that has sunk into terrifying darkness. There is nothing in it that would show a lost pilgrim the right direction. The forest begins to change, and the pilgrim says:

> I looked up and saw the peaks
> Which the sun had clothed with brightness
> That anyone can go straight to.[31]

The scene takes place at daybreak, and this early morning light enables the pilgrim to recognize threats in the form of animals (a leopard, a lion, and a wolf) and also to meet with Virgil, his guide, who ultimately leads him all the way to the boundary of the world that falls into the sphere of redemption. If we translate Badiou's understanding of the idea of communism into this Dantean scene of the dark forest, we discover another meaning. The hitherto unknown form of this idea creates the light of daybreak, in which we catch sight of the full extent of the danger around us, and we recognize intellectual and political figurations that could be our guides. This idea gives those who are lost a hint of the right direction.

How Does the Idea Affect Society?

We certainly cannot measure the idea of communism empirically, but the idea of equality represents a factor in realignments and divisions that has manifested in quite real ways in political, economic, and cultural history. The idea of communism created a certain gravitational field that was itself invisible from the perspective of existing power structures and their ideologies, but it still provoked political and social movement in a certain direction. In a specific situation: for example, in the period of the resistance movement in occupied France, an encounter with a representative of the communist resistance group could become a gateway into the gravitational field created by this idea—this is what Louis Althusser writes about his encounter with the communist Pierre Courrèges in a German prison camp. Althusser describes his entry into the gravitational field of communism in this way: "Though no one asked him to do so, Courrèges intervened off his own bat and in the cause of honesty and fraternity." He was "straightforward, direct, warm, and natural, and seemed capable of talking and acting quite effortlessly. His presence alone transformed the camp and we were totally astonished by him. All the accommodations and semi-compromises with the Germans disappeared overnight . . . "[32] This type of conduct had an irresistible effect on Althusser and converted him to communism. The idea of communism does not act like a natural law, but it is an exception that occurs in a certain situation and in certain intellectual and experiential compositions of individuals, and the effect of such an encounter cannot be predicted in advance. In the historical period when the idea of communism was active, this encounter could change into a connection with the community of "faithful subjects" that Badiou claims is searching for elements of this idea, and thus give it new and unpredictable meanings. In *Being and Event*, Badiou refers to this search connected with distinguishing situational elements as truth procedures and generic procedures.[33]

In *Logics of Worlds*, he introduces the concept of the evental presence, which is "the set of consequences of the evental trace" that are created by a sequence of singular decisions in the given situation.[34] The evental trace exists in the world when there is at least one faithful subject who makes a decision in relation to situational elements as an "operational unit." From this perspective, the faithful subject is a localization of truth because they develop the consequences of the truth in the given world and, in this way, the event leaves a trace in it.[35] The evental trace thus arises because of the faithful subject, and if the subject disintegrates, this trace also disappears from the world.

Badiou cites the example of Spartacus and the group of slaves who declared that they are returning to their homelands, from which they had been abducted as slaves. This event statement leads to a whole series of decisions. Should the slaves, who behave like free beings, create an army that takes a stand against the Romans? Where will they go? These decisions are usually a choice between yes and no in the end. Badiou terms them the "points" of the specific situation.[36] Spartacus's army forms a collective body that continues in the direction of the evental trace that was made with the declaration "We slaves want to and can go home." This body is gradually formed in individual points of decision. In a point decision of "yes–no," it can happen that the decision is not unanimous and the collective body of Spartacus's army appears as a body that is internally "barred" or split. For this event body, Badiou uses Lacan's symbol $ (*sujet barré*, the barred subject), with which Lacan expresses the ineradicable internal splitting of the subject. Badiou's symbol of an event body that has been split like this is ¢. However, the internal division that belongs to the character of the event body due to the necessity of its making point decisions does not mean that Spartacus's army breaks up into gangs that begin to pursue their own immediate group interests. Due to point decisions, the internal splitting of the collective body doesn't lead to its disintegration and fragmentation under the condition that this body acts as an "organ of presence," which is how Badiou refers to the ability of the collective body to integrate its elements into the presence. The runaway slave enters Spartacus's divisions, but in doing so he is incorporated in the presence into the actualization of a previously unknown possibility. He enters a new presence, in which there exists the possibility of returning home.[37]

Incorporation into the event body as an organ of the presence creates a form of unification that is not the result of a democratic acceptance of a majority decision, nor is it mere military obedience to a commander. Incorporation into the body of the presence creates a different type of cohesion that arises when an individual and his or her body become part of the faithful subject that develops the consequences of the evental trace. Thanks to this connection to the event subject, the individual moves in a new presence that transforms his relationship to his own physical body and its animalistic human conditionality. Badiou defines a new presence both by containing the evental trace and by possibilities appearing within it that had not existed before the occurrence of the evental trace because it was impossible to imagine them as real possibilities. The individual, as a part of the event subject, along with the others, is disposed to maintain and develop a unified form of this subject as an organ of presence, even though his voice in point decisions is not the same as the voice of the majority or the voice of the commander. As soon as this event subject ceases to be an organ or presence and it loses the capability of developing consequences of the evental trace, its disintegration into gangs or mutually quarreling group fragments can take place. The event subject changes into a mere plurality, in which the differences among individual elements produce greater effects than the mutual relationship to the evental trace.

Spartacus's army of slaves provides Badiou with an example of a collective body that maintains its presence despite its internal strife until its downfall, which was brought about by a betrayal by Sicilian pirates and by its military defeat. An example of a collective body that ceased to maintain its presence at a certain stage and began to have "liquidating" or "reactive" effects is the Communist Party. Badiou says that in the 1920s and 1930s, it was a political body that, during the period of workers' and people's mobilization, helped form a "public revolutionary consciousness." The Party did this, for instance, by supporting the anticolonial movement in the Arab world.[38] In the 1930s, the Communist Party in Germany displayed liquidating effects when it refused to cooperate with the Social Democrats. In France, from May 1968, anti-leftist attitudes and efforts to suppress the event nature of the year 1968 were another manifestation of it. The effects of the Communist Party were "reactive": it changed from a faithful subject that maintains its presence to a reactive subject that suppresses the presence, even though it still has the word "communist" in its name.

Transformation of the Communist Idea in Stalinist Platonism

Badiou only marginally deals with the extinction of evental traces and the transformation of the faithful subject into a reactive subject, which is understandable because his main themes were a defense of the very existence of truths and a demonstration that it is possible to create a faithful subject. He generally understands the transformation of the Communist Party into a reactive subject in this way: the Communist Party linked the idea of communism with the state and was therefore unable to prevent the state from absorbing the idea into itself. The state was only supposed to exist temporarily, in the interest of maintaining the results of the revolution. However, instead of the state withering away in the gravitational field of the communist idea, it became a rigid structure that transformed the idea of communism into one of its own elements. The incorporation of the idea of communism into the structure of the state meant that the idea lost its evental trace and began to be extinguished. Although it continued to exist within the structure of the state, for example in the form of "communist ideology," it was eventually extinguished to such an extent that it ended up in a frozen condition.

I associate the problem of the extinguishment and freezing of the idea of communism with Badiou's critique of Stalinism as a "depoliticization" of communism. Badiou mentions Mao's polemics with Stalinism and emphasizes that Stalin's fundamental error was his lack of faith in the masses, especially the peasantry. Stalinist depoliticization was caused by the fact that the state structure associated with the revolution in 1917 had lost the "determinants of political truths." Badiou then lists the four determinants that define the "generic core of political truth of this type." They are trust, which refuses to be suspicious of the masses; will, focused on socioeconomic necessity; equality, which works against established hierarchies in power and in the economy; and an authority that disrupts the "naturalness" of competition.[39] Badiou highlights Mao's critical words about Stalin's "objectivism" as a government of technology, cadres, and economic "laws," which was lacking the will to "become the masters of these laws."[40] We could conclude from this passage that Badiou understands Stalinism merely as a depoliticization that expresses capitulation to socioeconomic laws and confirms the power hierarchy that had emerged.

However, in the book *The Communist Hypothesis*, Badiou does attribute the ability to politicize to Stalinism. Here again, he relies on Mao, who considered Khrushchev's critique of Stalin's "cult of personality" as the beginning of the decline of the communist idea, which was to play out over the next decades. What Badiou meant by this was the symbol of proper names, which play an irreplaceable role in combining, unifying, and lending significance to "the anonymous action of millions of militants, rebels, fighters, unrepresentable as such."[41] It was necessary to criticize Stalin's terrorist conception of the state from the perspective of revolutionary politics, whereas for Badiou, Khrushchev's critique was an abstract rejection of the role of personal names in political subjectivization. Khrushchev's consumer humanism, expressed in the slogan "Everything for the good of man," bolstered a government made up of groups that had been in power under Stalin, and thus reinforced the state structure. The communist idea changed into a state ideology, which can be labeled "reactionary humanism."[42] It was Khrushchev who completed the depoliticization that was still incomplete under Stalinism. In Stalinism, a symbolic power of names operated that provoked a politicization of society, and it provided the communist idea with a modus operandi.

Another feature of Stalinism appears in Badiou's "Third Sketch of a Manifesto of Affirmationist Art" : the "Platonic dispositive," which acts as a "didactic" imperative of an idea that subordinates itself to art from the outside.[43] Badiou does not further elaborate on this motif; however, it would not be out of place to catch sight of a tension in Badiou's concept of Stalinism, which suggests that Stalinism is much more elusive and mysterious than it would appear from totalitarian interpretations. The Platonic dispositive and depoliticized objectivism appear to be opposites. Depoliticized objectivism expresses capitulation before the laws of empirical reality and before hierarchies of economy and power. However, the Stalinist imperative of the idea subordinates these givenness if we assume that the imperative is not only limited to art.

Badiou's verdict on Stalinism in the book *Logics of Worlds* is unequivocal: Stalinism is the depoliticized doctrine of a terrorist state in which the communist idea was extinguished. However, his statement in the *Communist Hypothesis* casts doubt on this unequivocal verdict. In Stalinism, the symbolic power of names was operating, and this gave labels to multifarious anonymous activities that were related to the idea of communism, but it is still the case that this symbolic power of names ceases to function in the next period. In the Prague Spring, the state structure becomes politicized and at least two "determinants of political truths" were renewed. The first was trust in the masses, which Dubček and the leaders of the communist party expressed in various ways (the demand for democratization, the abolition of censorship, and contact with people). And there was also equality against the established power and economic hierarchies, which was expressed by the expanding ranks of workers' councils operating in Czechoslovakia at that time.[44]

In Stalinism, there was a Platonic idea that differed from the communist idea, whose various collective embodiments created evental traces. In what way do the Stalinist Platonic idea and the truth-embodying communist idea differ? In the book *Logics of Worlds*, Badiou writes about an obscure subject that obscures the presence of evental traces by invoking an atemporal fetish of the Community, God, or the Race as an inviolable and indivisible transcendent entity that allegedly appeared in the past.[45] We can understand the Stalinist Platonic idea as a special variant of obscure formations, even though Badiou does not call it this. It is properly classified as an obscure formation because it reveals an immediate fullness that has a fictitious and atemporal character.[46] Its meaning is not transformed in relation to the variable elements that occur in individual time-conditioned situations, as is the case with a truth procedure. An example of this obscure character of Stalinism is the rejection of cooperation with the German Social Democrats in the period when Nazism was on the rise. The fatal refusal to work together with this antifascist party was justified by ideological purity. In the obscure light of the Platonic idea, the Social Democrats appeared impure due to their cooperation with capital, which liberally provided it with social legitimization. The obscure purity of the Stalinist idea caused the defeat of mutually isolated antifascist parties and facilitated the victorious advancement of Nazism. However, the Stalinist Platonic idea is specific in that the place from which it comes is not a fictitious past, as is the case with other obscure formations, but rather a fictitious future. It is an idea that expresses the immediate fullness of the conception of the future communist society.

The obscure character of the Stalinist idea can be explained as the result of a fetishization of Marxist concepts. We can find a description of this in Sartre. This thinker explains conceptual fetishization as a regression of Marxism, which was the tragic outcome of the besiegement the Soviet Union found itself in during the 1920s and 1930s, in an ebb phase of the world revolutionary movement. In this period, the Soviet Union was internationally isolated and launched into a massive industrialization of the country. Its ideology is subordinated to the requirement of "security," which is understood as unity, and the requirement of "building socialism."[47] Sartre thus explains the origin of the fetishization as a consequence of adverse historical circumstances.

Sartre and Badiou are in agreement here: both of them interpret Stalinism mainly in relation to the Soviet Union's isolation. An essentially irresolvable aporia arose, which posed the question of whether to continue in the international tendency with the goal of provoking revolution in the advanced Western countries, or to focus instead on defending the results of the revolution in one country. This was an aporia between revolutionary experiments and the requirement of self-preservation. The first way was part of what Lenin and Trotsky intended, and hypothetically could bring complex assistance from the Western countries into backward Russia, and these countries would take inspiration from Russia in heading toward socialism themselves. However, owing to the influence of the consolidation of relations in the Western countries in the 1920s, this was never a realistic plan. The second path can be seen as an understandable response to the retreat of revolutionary movements in western Europe and to the rise of militant nationalism in Germany. The very survival of the Soviet state in a backward country and in the unfavorable international conditions was the highest priority. Badiou writes that the party-state acted as an operator of a violent economic and social transformation of the country. The dictatorship of the proletariat was understood as a depoliticized domination of the state, which had to exert enormous pressure on accelerating the growth of production. According to Badiou, the masses were enthusiastic for this program and threw themselves into it, but it was not an enthusiasm for the "political work," as he labels the creations that arise in the course of the development of the generic idea of communism in the book *The Immanence of Truths*.[48] This colossal program lacked a historical model that would show what to beware of, so it was impossible to avoid making mistakes. However, the problems and difficulties that arose were blamed on traitors and fascists—which Badiou claimed happened because the party-state had been depoliticized. Owing to the objectivism of the economic goals, the power structure no longer transformed and it wasn't possible to subject it to criticism. Difficulties and problems were not put into connection with the political system of the party-state, but instead were blamed on individuals or various social groups. According to Badiou, this depoliticization was the cause of the terrorist tactics used by the Stalinist party-state, which disrupted or suffocated the effects of the generic communist idea. However, at the same time, Badiou also points out that a symbolic power of names maintained the political effectiveness of this idea of equality among the ranks of nameless activists. Badiou's concept of Stalinism thus isn't in contradiction with more recent historical research that is discovering a dynamic dialectic between the party-state and the common people, who reacted in unpredictable ways to state-organized campaigns. The research in this area indicates that a relationship emerged between politics "from above" and politics "from below" which manifested, for example, in laborers using egalitarian slogans from party campaigns against the bosses of the enterprises where they were employed. These managers were starting to form a new caste, so the state apparatus had to react to the complaint.[49]

In this situation, the fetishization of Marxist concepts, which according to Sartre, had been brought about by the demands for "unity" and for "building socialism" as two regulative principles in the Soviet Union's domestic politics during the period of its international isolation. In Sartre's opinion, Marxist fetishism arose as a result of ruling politicians' fear of the development of a truth that wasn't constrained by anything at all, which can be termed a "generic procedure" in Badiou's terminology. In their eyes, this truth could undermine the unity that gave the party its fighting power. Therefore, they began to determine the general lines and interpretations of events themselves. The imperative of unity, which was brought into practice through the exercise of power in making decisions, caused the loss of what Badiou calls the "determinants of political truth," which mainly meant a loss of trust in the masses, which are the site of various forms of development of truth procedures and their perpetual renewal. The power imperative of unity gave rise to processes in which concepts such as "the working class" became rigid ideas that were isolated from experience. Sartre writes that "people and things were a priori subordinated to ideas."[50] Stalinist Platonic ideas are the result of a conceptual fetishization in which Sartre recognized two simultaneous operations. The first is "conceptualization," in which an empirical concept pretends to be a complete type that expresses the "formal unity of abstract and universal relations."[51] The concept "the working class" captures a certain empirical aspect, but the character of this concept is Platonic. Its content is separated from a truth procedure that develops in the ambiguous data of experience. According to Sartre, the fetishistic concept expresses a "general singularity," in which the originally empirical element becomes an entirely abstract concept that lacks an immediate relation to experience. The second operation is the "border crossing." This is where the fetishization culminates, because the real power to negate its opposite or any foreign adulteration is attributed to the concept. A real existence is attributed to "the working class," which negates any qualities that don't correspond to the abstract concept of it. As an example, Sartre cites the idea of "democracy of workers' councils," which carries an absolute negation of bureaucracy with it. He speaks of the Marxist terms that various parties have used in interpreting the Hungarian uprising in 1956. This process of fetishization does not only apply to Stalinist concepts but also to the Marxist concepts used by Trotskyites and in the anarcho-communism of the "workers' councils." According to Sartre, Marxist fetishistic concepts have an atemporal character similar to Badiou's obscure formations. Their content cannot be disrupted by the pluralistic processes taking place in society. There is a gap which I term "fetishistic chorism" between them and the pluralistic social processes. It is precisely through this gap that fetishistic Platonism differs from Badiou's truth procedures, which are established by the movement in search of the plurality substance of the given situation, whose result cannot be known in advance.

The question of a more general meaning is therefore whether conceptual fetishization is not a general tendency in the modern and postmodern eras that applies to all concepts that become part of political or economic practice. The process of fetishization did not only occur with concepts such as communism and the working class; it also took place with concepts that are building blocks of liberal democracy and neoliberal economics. "Freedom," "democracy," and "the market" display the characteristics of conceptual fetishes that are also isolated from pluralistic experience. The manifestation of this fetishization is the fact that no phenomenon or experience can refute the belief that our political system is a democracy, although according to Lucian Canfora, it is easy to prove that we live in a disproportionately mixed system that could be described as an oligarchy with elements of democracy.[52] In his studies of practice from the late 1960s, and mainly in his "Marginalia to Theory and Practice," Adorno points out that the state of the technical forces of production, along with the enduring principle of domination, causes a reversal of goals and means.[53] Economic progress becomes a goal that has a fetishistic character, while the all-around liberation of humankind and reconciliation of civilization with nature—which emancipation theory considered to be the goal of economic progress—appear to be obstruction or resistance. From these studies by Adorno, it can be concluded that economic categories (such as the market) have been disconnected from the theory that used to see the means to another goal through economics, and they have taken on the nature of conceptual fetishes that are reminiscent of the Stalinist Platonic idea in a certain sense.

In liberal-democratic practice, "freedom" and "democracy" are subjected not only to fetishistic conceptualization but also to the second operation that Sartre called the border crossing. The way this manifests is that first a real existence is ascribed to these concepts; then, empowered in this way, freedom and democracy negate any qualities that are in contradiction with their abstract definitions. Fetishized freedom and democracy draw a line, or boundary marker, between "freedom" and "democracy" and whatever doesn't correspond to their pure conception. This results in the exclusion and negation of everything that disrupts the "pure" ideas of freedom and democracy, such as populism. As conceptual fetishes, "freedom" and "democracy" begin, with their atemporal character, to resemble the Platonic ideals of the type that the idea of communism had transformed into during the Stalinist period. Stalinist Platonic ideas can be considered a kind of anticipation of the forms that the concepts of "freedom," "democracy," and "the market" took on in political and economic practice. In his work, Badiou shows that there are exceptions to these fetishizations, but they are not protected from the fetishization taking place within them. In the nineteenth and twentieth centuries, there was a politics that took the form of a truth procedure, and its concepts developed into the plurality of elements of individual situations. It was a politics that formed evental traces and maintained their presence, despite pressure for them to be absorbed by the party-state.

Only now is the connection coming to light between Badiou's characteristics of Stalinism that appear to be opposite: Stalinism as an objectivism of economic laws, and Stalinism as an imperative Platonic ideal. The objectivism of economic laws can be understood as the reversal of means and goals that Adorno was writing about. Building socialism becomes the goal to which even the theory that speaks about the building of economic socialism not being a goal in itself but a means for creating an emancipated society has been subordinated. The fetishization of the construction of socialism, as described by Sartre, is taking place here, and its result is an imperative of the Platonic ideal of "building socialism." This imperative commands us to submit to the objectivism of economic laws, and this submission or capitulation is understood as a necessary condition for building socialism. The Stalinist Platonic ideal of "building socialism" is a result of the conceptual fetishization and has an obscure character in the sense described above. We can therefore term a subject that identifies with the Stalinist Platonic ideal as an obscure subject.

Badiou writes that the obscure subject offers "the chance of a new destiny, under the incomprehensible but salvific sign of an absolute body."[54] However, he does not introduce a term that would express the relationship between the obscure subject and this absolute body. An obscure analogy of trust in the subject, which is connected with the truth procedure, is operating here. This obscure relationship can evoke an enthusiasm that may be stronger than it is in a faithful subject. This is because the attachment to the obscure object, which can be understood as a fetishistic Platonic ideal, is inaccessible to questioning of the various elements of the specific situation in which the truth procedure is operating. The Stalinist procedure limits or abolishes "determinants of political truth," and the obscure idea of communism takes precedence over the truth idea of communism. The conceptual fetishization and the emergence of the Platonic obscure idea create Stalinist enthusiasm, which can be explained by "conceptualization" and "border" crossing taking place here, during which this idea is isolated from the plurality of moments that would disrupt their purity. A real power is attributed to this pure idea, which then purges society of those who fail to correspond to its ideal definition. Due to the influence of this fetishization, the obscure idea of communism, to which the Stalinist subject is attached, is protected from doubts and the uncertainty of searching, and it offers a seductively immediate connection or identification. And through such fetishistic operations, Stalinism became a source of unadulterated enthusiasm, which strengthened its bearers in their conviction that the name of Stalin is a guarantee of the truth of the communist idea.

May 1968, the Chinese Cultural Revolution, the Prague Spring, and the Extinction of the Idea of Communism

Stalinism was a crucial period in the past sequence of the communist idea. During this time, it transformed into a Platonic ideal that almost completely suppressed its truth procedure, even though a complete extinguishment did not take place. The years 1968–78 witnessed the final phase of this sequence, in which the idea took on new forms, while at the same time also showing its practical ineffectiveness. These were mainly experiments with a type of politics that appeared in the anti-system movement in 1968. According to Badiou, this politics appeared in a concentrated form in May 1968 in France, where the radical student movement joined with workers and employees, and—independent of political parties—they nearly provoked an anti-system revolution. They culminated in a general strike that forced President de Gaulle to leave the country. Badiou writes that May 1968 was the last time when all the participating groups were using a unified symbol: the color red. This symbolism expressed affiliation with the Marxist politics that began with the October Revolution. All the actors were speaking the same language, whether they were orthodox Marxists, radical leftists (*gauchistes*), Maoists, or Trotskyites. All of them were using a vocabulary that contained expressions such as class, class struggle, proletarian leadership of the struggle, although there were disagreements and conflicts over how to politically concretize these terms.[55] However, the "secret truth" of the 1968 movement was that these generally used Marxist terms had already begun to die out in practical politics. The following ten years of political experiments showed that this vocabulary had lost its political meaning, but no new vocabulary was available. In these "red years," as Badiou terms them, traditional unions and established political parties turned out to be obstacles to anti-system politics, which had the goal of finding a strategy that would unblock the barricaded path to an all-around emancipation of society. Badiou describes the understanding of communism among the 1968 activists and the following "red" decade as the concept of a society where the airtight walls and barriers that separated various social positions were torn down. Communism was supposed to offer variable values, life goals, and opportunities to realize oneself at work.[56] The new left of that period questioned the established positions and various types of social hierarchy. They considered parliamentary politics to be ineffective, and on the basis of experience with the French Communist Party in 1968, they also perceived it as a tool that serves to pacify the revolutionary social movement. The slogan of 1968 was: "Elections are a con."[57] During this period, political experiments with non-parliamentary activism, as Badiou says, proved unable to discover a new form of political organization that could avoid both disintegrative anarchy and organizational ossification. And despite all the efforts, this form still has not been found to this day.[58] May 1968 represents a "nameless" event whose consequences are unclear and scattered, which makes creating a unifying name for it impossible. In Badiou's view, many activists and theorists had realized even then that a period of emancipatory politics had closed—they didn't have to wait until 1989.

According to Badiou, the second event that concluded this sequence was the Cultural Revolution in China (1965–76). The Cultural Revolution was a reference point for anti-system activities worldwide, and it had an especially significant impact in France from 1967 to 1977. The French 1968 movement and ensuing political experiments were inspired in many regards by the Chinese Cultural Revolution, and Badiou himself was part of the Maoist faction. He describes its influence as inspiring the activists of that time to change their subjectivity, their lives, and their thinking.[59] Badiou also argues that this was the revolution that showed with finality that the communist idea cannot be renewed within the framework of a party-state. Neither the extraordinary political creativity of students and working people (1966–8), nor the ideological and state control by the army (1968–71), nor the ad hoc solutions adopted by the Politburo (1972–6) proved able to accomplish the goal of the Cultural Revolution, which was to create an "entirely new political situation, completely detached from the Soviet model."[60] The Cultural Revolution failed because the movement from below was unable to create forms of organization at the national level that would effectively replace the structure of the party-state. The elimination of a centralized party leadership led to an anarchic division of the movement into smaller and smaller fractions, and a movement divided in this way was unable to gain control over the chaos in the economy and state administration. This chaos then allowed party cadres to come into power, and they then introduced market-based economic reforms.[61]

Badiou sees the Chinese Cultural Revolution as the starting point for seeking a new form of the communist idea in the twenty-first century; one that is going to address the question of whether it is possible to have politics without a party.[62] In order to facilitate a better understanding of this reference point of Badiou's, it is necessary to mention that the protests in Tiananmen Square in Beijing in 1989 were an example of the application of certain elements of the Cultural Revolution. According to Shen Tong, one of the student leaders, the fuse that lit the fire was handwritten posters with large characters (*dazibao*) that had been used during the Cultural Revolution as a form of public discussion. Shen Tong writes that the expressions of hostility from local populations that groups of students encountered were similar to what the student Red Guards experienced during the Cultural Revolution.[63] The protests had four basic goals: democracy, freedom of expression, economic equality, and the elimination of corruption. This protest movement did not see democracy as the proclamation of free elections and the introduction of a Western parliamentary system, but rather as citizens' political participation.[64] There was not a direct link between them and the Cultural Revolution, but in the different position they found themselves after Deng Xiaoping's introduction of market reforms, the protests aimed at analogous goals to those of the Cultural Revolution: the political activation of society from below, the elimination of privileges for the party elite, and the reduction of economic inequality. The symbolic expression of these goals was that the protesting students and workers in China in 1989 sang the Internationale, just like they had during the Cultural Revolution.

However, the Prague Spring of 1968 should be considered the third event that concludes this sequence. Badiou understood it as a "weak form" of attempts to resolve the contradictions of emancipatory politics of the twentieth century.[65] He did not appreciate that in the Prague Spring a dialectical relationship took shape between the party-state and the mass social movement that had been lacking in the Chinese Cultural Revolution. In the Prague Spring, interactions were initiated between the party and the mass movement that was created through workers' councils in factories, spontaneous speeches by the people, local initiatives, and other activities from below. These interactions set both poles into motion, and—on the basis of the mutual feedback—they began to change. The reform thus turned into a revolution that had no prototype in history, as Gordon Skilling claims in his book *Czechoslovakia's Interrupted Revolution*.[66] Both of the poles arrived at a historically unresearched terrain in which previously untried forms of emancipatory politics appeared.[67] In this reform, which turned into a revolution, spontaneity combined with a consolidation of the results already achieved through the state's mediation. This process did not lead to the chaos that the Chinese Cultural Revolution found itself in, and—on the contrary—there was spontaneity in it that prevented its stagnation. Unlike the Chinese Cultural Revolution, the Prague Spring did not end up trapped in the dead end Badiou writes about. Political, social, economic, and legal conceptions that reacted to existing problems and dialectically connected potentially antagonistic tendencies were developed. A political model of socialist democracy was emerging, in which a centralized government, direct democracy, and common ownership of the means of production (socialism) were to be combined; a conception of market socialism connected with a central coordination of the economy was created; and there appeared proposals for the institutional and constitutionally guaranteed provision for the existence of socialism, which would enable the abolishment of the communist party without leading to a restoration of capitalism.[68] These, and other conceptions suggested that although the Prague Spring was taking a difficult and previously untried path, it would not end up in a dead end as the Chinese Cultural Revolution had.

In the Prague Spring, the hidden possibilities of the communist sequence of that time appeared. This was at a time when the idea of communism had already transformed into an ideological element of the state structure, but the Prague Spring showed that it could be revived as a truth procedure. The Prague Spring was suppressed by the state structure of the Soviet Union and other Warsaw Pact countries, where the revival of the truth procedure appeared like an eccentric deviation from the established order of things—and one that threatened the very existence of the Eastern Bloc. As the apt title of Skilling's books suggests, this was a revolution that was interrupted from the outside. In the context of this communist sequence, the end of the Prague Spring is, therefore, perhaps a more significant symbolic watershed than the political ebbing of the significance of the events in France after 1968. The Prague Spring was a call for a revolutionary reform of the Soviet-type state structure, which came from within this structure, whereas May 1968 in France was a challenge issued to the capitalist state. May 1968 revealed the ossification of the communist idea in the Soviet bloc only indirectly by the Communist Party of France, in conformity with the Soviet Union's foreign policy, refusing a general strike and other actions taken by the student and workers' movement.

I call the years 1968–78 or, more broadly, 1968–89, the period of the extinguishing of the communist idea. An interregnum has not yet appeared in the proper sense of the term, as events transpire that still relate to the communist sequence that began in 1917, and they are searching for a new modality. Badiou makes particular mention of the Polish Solidarity movement, in which a mass-based workers' movement stood up against the bureaucratic state apparatus in the name of socialism. Other examples include Chile during President Allende's administration, certain movements in South America and in the Near East, Arab socialism in Libya, and the Maoists in Nepal after 1989. At the same time, there are experiments with politics without a party and outside of a state, which separate themselves from this communist sequence and are instead typical of the initial period of an interregnum. Badiou offers the first two years of the Portuguese revolution, the first stage of the Iranian revolution against the Shah, the Political Organization in France, and the Zapatista movement in Mexico, which appeared after 1989, as examples.[69]

During this period, the states of the Eastern Bloc became structures where the idea of communism existed in a mummified form, like a dead body surrounded by empty symbols and accompanied by mechanical linguistic expressions. Or we can compare late state socialism to a refrigerator in which the idea of communism is preserved like a frozen body that has not turned into a skeleton, but which no one is able to revive. An example of this is the television series *Gottwald* (1986, dir. E. Sokolovský), which was supposed to revive the founding ideals of the post-February regime, which are embodied by Klement Gottwald in the series. However, instead of reviving these ideals, the series provoked ironic reactions and ridicule: reruns were not broadcast. Here, the idea of communism existed as a frozen outer shell with the life extinguished within. As soon as thawing began in this state structure, such as during Gorbachev's perestroika, the idea of communism could not be revived as a truth procedure because it had begun to disintegrate.

During the period of its extinguishing, the communist idea ceased to function in the political and social sphere as an authoritative and formative factor. The year 1989 was only a symbolic closure for its extinguishment, although at that time, in the last brief sputters, a few of its elements came back to life a little, such as the idea of solidarity and socialism with a human face, whose significant role in the Czechoslovak "revolution with a human face" was documented by James Krapfl.[70] In the period of the extinguishing of the communist idea, the empty space began to be occupied by various conceptions, doctrines, and ideologies that set down roots in the social space where its traces had not yet cooled off. Marxist politics was dead, but Marx's spirit still hovered in the air, to use Jacques Derrida's expression.[71] In examining the first phase of the interregnum, this constellation is crucial because its characteristic traits are formed within it. Samuel Moyn writes that the political space of the 1970s began to be filled with human rights, which replaced the previous emancipatory ideals.[72] The human rights agenda was pursued with such urgency then because it was a replacement for the fading project of radical human emancipation. The political energy that was provoked by revolutionary and national-emancipatory movements, which didn't have other outlets after they weakened and died out, was projected into them. Moyn links the dissolution of Marxist revolutionary politics to the rise of the politics of human rights that began in the 1970s, thus touching on a more general phenomenon that has not yet been given due attention.

Badiou's periodization of the concept of the communist idea opens up not only a new perspective on human rights but also on economics, politics, and culture that were coming into being during the period of its extinguishing and became the dominant feature of the first period of the interregnum. These dominant features were neoliberalism, liberal democracy, and postmodernism. These are usually understood as constituting unique doctrines, forms of governance, normative systems, or cultural configurations that define themselves against the socialism or communism of the twentieth century, which is figured as totalitarianism, or a unifying grand narrative. If we realize that these dominating features arose in a period in which the radical emancipatory movements and social visions were fading away, we can start to ask whether there aren't any secret ties to the communist idea contained within them. We typically look at these dominant features from the opposite side, which is our current situation. Neoliberalism, liberal democracy, and postmodernism then appear to be colossi that have displaced the strange specters that occupied the social space before them. If we look at them as finished entities, the question does not come into our minds of whether these colossi have not drawn at least part of their ethos and political energy from a relationship to various embodiments of the communist idea in the twentieth century. This relationship necessarily overlaps. Neoliberalism, liberal democracy, and postmodernism ceased to depend on their source, and they attempted to suffice with only their own energy. It was only then that they began to appear like colossi that had at some time driven the specters away. Their dependency on period embodiments of the communist idea begins to show itself when we sketch out the situation in which they arose. This is how we can distinguish the roots of the first phase of the interregnum.

The Interregnum and Its Periods

We can define the beginning of the historical period that I refer to as the interregnum with the symbolic date of 1989. This is the year when the collapse of the Eastern Bloc confirmed quite manifestly that the sequence of the communist idea that was tied to the October Revolution as its founding event had ended. Along with Badiou, I consider the years 1968–78 to be the *practical* conclusion of this sequence, which was revealed by the experience with the political ineffectiveness of Marxism and its vocabulary in specific struggles in France, in China, and elsewhere in the world. In this period, the process of the communist idea's extinguishment, which had already begun in Stalinism when the party-state transformed the communist idea into a fetishistic Platonic idea and its truth procedure practically came to a standstill, continued. In this broader sense, the period actually lasted from the 1930s until 1989, and until 1968, there were still ideas and experiments cropping up that were able to renew the political effectiveness of the communist idea and reshape it. Already between 1968 and 1978, it was clear that the communist idea had lost its effectiveness, but until 1989—or even longer—it had its last reverberations in the social space, as evidenced by the "revolution with a human face" in November 1989. From 1968 to 1989, when the idea of communism was extinguished, the dominant ideas of the interregnum: neoliberalism, liberal democracy, and postmodernism took shape and took root.

I divide the interregnum's development to date into two periods. In its first period, the interregnum was shaped by neoliberalism, liberal democracy, and postmodernism: at that time, fragments of political and artistic truths were still lingering in a special substituted form, preventing the dominant features of the first phase of the interregnum (e.g., the market, individual freedom, singularity, and radical plurality) from merging with other elements (of various origins) that later caused these features to fissure and mutate. In this book, I deal with neoliberal conceptions and postmodern theories that mostly originated before 1989, but they only began to act as dominant influences afterward. In the conclusion of Part One of the book, I represent the overall characteristics of these two dominant features using the form of an epicycloid, which illustrates the relative positioning of the concepts and principles within these features. I therefore refer to the first period as epicyclic. Its duration is bounded by the year 1989 as the symbolic victory of neoliberalism and liberal democracy and 2008, when the worldwide financial crisis erupted and brought mass protests against the ossification of liberal democracy into a government by a "political caste." The turn of the new millennium marked a certain milestone for postmodernism, when its end was proclaimed by certain artists and cultural theorists.

The interregnum then has a second period, which began in 2008 and continues to this day. This is when neoliberalism and liberal democracy came into crisis and postmodernism ceased to function as a dominating element in culture. As we can see in the second section of Part One of the book, in the current period we no longer find any concepts and principles that occupy a central position. Evidence of what many have suspected appears: the present period has no center. In economics, there is a linkage of market individualism and self-sacrifice for the whole; in politics, individual freedom is connected with collective identities and populism; and in culture, postmodern irony is intertwined with a new seriousness and a desire for another world. In the contemporary economy, politics, and culture, there is a circulation between opposing principles and concepts, none of which forms a center. I have proposed an ellipse, which represents an eccentric form with two foci as an abstract model of these circulations, and therefore I characterize the present period as a transformation from epicycloids into an ellipse.

An examination of previous periods makes sense because it facilitates the understanding of the character of the present situation in the economy, politics, and culture. Understanding the present situation in its general features is one of the key tasks for emancipatory thinking. Recognizing the general features of individual phenomena makes it possible to stand at a distance from a specific situation that appears at that moment as a given, and a change to which—even if it's actively induced—is inconceivable. By generalizing, we distance ourselves from the immediate experience of the given, which is a necessary condition to break the spell of the myth that our fate is inevitable. No one expressed this emancipatory meaning of generalization better than Jameson when he wrote that "historical reconstruction, then, the positing of global characterizations and hypotheses, the abstraction from the 'blooming, buzzing confusion' of immediacy, was always a radical intervention in the here and now and the promise of resistance to its blind fatalities."[73]

Part One

The Eccentric Interregnum

Section One

The Epicyclic Period (1989–2000/2008)

1

Neoliberalism with Traces of Communism

Neoliberalism Proclaims Human Rights

Neoliberalism is usually seen as a comprehensive economic doctrine and form of politics distinguished by straightforward concepts and principles such as the free market, privatization, competition, deregulation, reduction of government expenditures, and commodification. Most supporters and opponents of neoliberal economic policy agree on its basic definition and its goal, which is a free market, unlimited by state interventions, in which an economic order should form spontaneously. Neoliberalism is usually conceived as an amoral doctrine that subordinates all values to economic calculations. As Jessica Whyte recently demonstrated, this idea of neoliberalism as economic reductionism overlooks the fact that for the founders of neoliberal thinking, free market competition was not only an effective technology for distributing goods and services but above all also a guarantee of individual rights and freedoms.[1] Friedrich Hayek did not agree with a purely economic understanding of the free market as a path to productivity and efficiency. In his eyes, the market replaced politics, where tendencies toward violence, coercion, and despotism were always being born. Market morality gave "the distant hope of a universal order of peace."[2] Hayek subscribed to the ideals of the French Revolution, such as the inalienable rights of man and the individual. The slogan "freedom, equality, and brotherhood" expressed rights that were interrelated with market competition. According to Hayek, these rights created market competitiveness because they ensured the inalienability of the individual's property as a result of his use of them in competition.[3] Whyte explains in detail that human rights are not an external appendage to neoliberalism, which can be accepted in some neoliberal politics and refused in others. On the contrary, human rights make up a part of neoliberalism because the neoliberal "founding fathers" saw them as an expression of market morality. As the author demonstrates, social democrats, socialists, and those who fought against colonialism understood human rights as being in contradiction to the ideas about human rights promoted by neoliberals. Human rights included demands for social security, national self-determination, and racial equality. Neoliberal human rights arise out of the conviction that "civil society" as a realm of freedom, voluntary cooperation, and expanded private power has control over politics, which is characterized by conflicts and limitations. The neoliberal conception of human rights became hegemonic. As Whyte relates, large humanitarian NGOs, such as Amnesty International, Human Rights Watch, and Doctors Without Borders, have adopted the neoliberal conception of human rights, which espouses the idea of civil society and defends individual rights and freedoms, while only rarely defending social policies and public services. The increased prominence of human rights in the 1970s is related to the change in rhetoric in the Cold War. In this period, the struggle between capitalism and communism was no longer understood as a competition in the economic and social spheres, and it was shifted to a political conflict between "repression and totalitarianism" and freedom and human rights.[4]

The rise of human rights in the 1970s allowed neoliberalism to become the dominant economic doctrine. In the Introduction, which was dedicated to the prehistory of the interregnum, we saw that the 1970s was the period of the extinction of the communist idea, which manifested in the decline and demise of radically emancipatory politics and national liberation movements. Samuel Moyn claims that the politics of human rights fills in this empty space and replaces the ideals that emancipation movements fought for in the 1950s and 1960s. Whyte is certainly right when she writes that human rights were part of neoliberalism since its beginnings in the 1930s, and especially since the founding of the Mont Pelerin Society that Friedrich Hayek established in 1947. However, neoliberalism asserted itself in the 1970s, using not only its conception of human rights but also ideas, principles, and practices that represented something like free radicals in the social environment of the time. These were the smoldering remains of the radical emancipatory movements of 1968—elements that were bound to more general principles connected with the idea of communism in the twentieth century.

How Neoliberalism Reshaped the Spirit of 1968

In their book *The New Spirit of Capitalism*, Luc Boltanski and Ève Chiapello speak about the absorption of radical ideals of 1968 by neoliberal capitalism. These were still part of class politics in the mid-1970s, and Mitterrand's government considered extending them in the beginning of the 1980s when it sought to deprivatize strategically important enterprises.[5] These authors illustrate in detail how neoliberalism exploited the ideals of 1968 and semantically shifted them. The demand for economic participation was translated into the language of corporate management as an expansion of employee stockholding.[6] The demand for economic democracy was translated into a trend toward nonauthoritative business management, in which semiautonomous working groups were going to participate in decision-making. The idea of self-government as a substitute for economic autonomy spread throughout companies and society.[7] Another ideal that was transformed in this way was the conception of a network as an expression of dynamic and nonhierarchical relations that tore down the walls that separate individual places in society. The ideal of flexibility, which expressed the demand for relaxation of social and cultural identities created by the capitalist order, also had a transformed expression.

It is necessary to correct Whyte in one thing: in the 1970s and thereafter, neoliberalism did not only limit itself to human rights (which the neoliberal authors considered to be concerned with individual rights and freedoms) but it also connected itself to the spirit of 1968, refashioning some of its elements managerially and absorbing them in this form. Its connection to the spirit of 1968 and the incorporation of the elements that had been transformed by capitalism was one of the reasons why society changed remarkably quickly in Western countries. Neoliberal politicians began winning elections, and neoliberalism became a hegemonic economic doctrine. Thanks to the neoliberal transformation of the spirit of 1968, a society rife with strikes and class-based manifestations of resistance changed into one focused on individual life goals, with an obliging and conciliatory attitude toward employers prevailing. In Western countries, an average of 4 million strike days can be counted in the years from 1971 to 1975, compared with only half a million in 1992.[8] As Badiou claims, the ideas, demands, and political approaches in 1968 were attempting to embody the idea of communism, loosely connected to 1917, but ultimately it turned out that its modifications had been exhausted. Neoliberalism, in the period of the final extinguishment of the idea of communism, absorbed its fragments into itself and transformed them into the form of new managerial practices and capitalist values. Neoliberalism thus created concepts and values (nonauthoritarian management, popular shareholding, relationship networks, self-management, flexibility), which complemented the individualism of rights and freedoms that had already been proclaimed by neoliberal authors.

However, they were not only fragments of 1968. Neoliberalism was also able to utilize other egalitarian imperatives of the communist idea that had been introduced into society by radical emancipatory movements, in mutated forms. Neoliberal theorists and politicians have always drawn a strict line against socialism and communism, where they perceived state despotism, the suppression of individual rights and freedoms, a politics of conflict, and even a threat to human civilization. In neoliberalism, however, we see a certain distinction between political forms and conceptual elements that relate to socialism and communism. Neoliberals rejected socialism and communism in the form of a directive state economy, political controls, and the bureaucratic subjugation of the individual. However, neoliberalism did adopt some egalitarian political practices, which Badiou connects with the communist truth procedure, and it imprinted its own form upon them.

Egalitarian elements can be found in the neoliberal politics of the 1980s and 1990s. The extensive privatization and deregulation that formed the basis of Margaret Thatcher's neoliberal politics in the 1980s were accompanied by a peculiar capitalist ethos of equality. In 1980, Thatcher enacted the "Housing Act," which allowed municipal apartments to be transferred to the private ownership of their residents. The slogan was that the British would be a nation where everyone would own the place where they lived. Citizens would then be equal in owning their housing as their personal property. Another egalitarian motif can be found in the privatization program that divided state-owned enterprises into shares intended for employees and small investors. Thatcher promised that the British would become a nation of stockholders.[9] Most citizens would be equal by becoming stockholders, and therefore capitalists. Neoliberal egalitarianism connected citizenship with capitalist ownership in an opposite manner than it had been done in the nineteenth-century period of liberal capitalism. At that time, property ownership was a condition for full civil rights: there was a property qualification clause that caused the poor to be deprived of the right to vote. Marx and the socialists therefore criticized the bourgeois political freedom that was limited only to property owners and excluded society's poor majority. And at the beginning of the twentieth century, the socialist movement insisted upon universal suffrage and a universal conception of citizenship. Under the influence of these egalitarian achievements, neoliberalism inverted the relationship between citizenship and ownership: citizenship thus became a guarantee of access to ownership. Thatcher promised every citizen that she would give them the possibility of becoming an owner. This egalitarian principle can be called capitalized citizenship.

Egalitarian motifs were also used in the Czech coupon privatization. The basic idea behind this project was that there would be a lightning strike on state ownership, which would make citizens into shareholders in Czech and Czechoslovak enterprises. State ownership was quickly privatized so that every citizen had the chance to buy an ownership share in a certain enterprise for a symbolic fee. In this way, the coupon privatization program transformed the project of economic democracy that had been realized during the Prague Spring. Although the authors of the coupon privatization scheme explicitly rejected the conception of the Prague Spring, they declared the idea that stock ownership is for everyone, which was de facto a transformed version of the socialist participation of employees in managing enterprises during the Prague Spring. As stated above, socialism in the form of economic democracy and self-governance was one of the visions that influenced ideas and programs in the period of a "revolution with a human face" in 1989. In the early 1990s, Václav Klaus and other neoliberal politicians were the only relevant political actors who were able to work with this egalitarian economic expectation, and they imprinted a form upon it that was in keeping with the individualistic principles of neoliberalism. Through this capitalist transformation of the egalitarian economic projects of 1968, they won most of society over to their side and achieved a convincing electoral victory. This project soon began to act as a means to effectuate the swift accumulation and concentration of property that some of those who were involved in it speak about in the documentary film *Česká cesta* [The Czech Way] (2015, dir. M. Kohout). However, the coupon privatization proves that neoliberalism used the revived fragments of the communist idea to promote its own main goals.

Neoliberalism attributes a certain role to the state. As Jessica Whyte emphasizes, criticism of economic interventions by the state does not mean that neoliberalism rejects political principles and state institutions. Neoliberalism learned from the mistakes of liberalism in the nineteenth and first half of the twentieth centuries and eliminated the naïve faith that the invisible hand of the market doesn't need any institutions in order to create a spontaneous order. Hayek and neoliberal thinkers generally agree that the market can't function without the rule of law, which guarantees the inalienability of individual human rights and freedoms. But Whyte points out that the state has a broader meaning than merely guaranteeing property rights in neoliberalism. Neoliberal thinking is based on the assumption that the institutional framework significantly influences market operations, though it does not arise from them. The state should be active in ensuring the conditions for market development, but it should not compensate losses caused by the market.[10] This etatist feature of neoliberalism had already been noted by Claus Offe in the 1980s, when he wrote that the state in the period of the crisis of the social state carries out "administrative recommodification." The state encourages the transnational integration of capital, which then increases the pressure to "heal" that country's economy, and part of the economy is deliberately left altogether without any protection in order to expose it to the immediate effects of the market.[11] Neoliberal politics as an administrative recommodification differs from the classical liberal doctrine of laissez-faire and doesn't reject the state as such, but only state redistribution of the results of market competition and other forms of disruption of market relations. This conception of the state reflects experience with unregulated capitalism that led to the worldwide economic crisis in the 1930s, which then strengthened authoritarian movements and undermined the legitimacy of the market and capitalism as such for long decades afterward. This shaken confidence in the market and in capitalism enabled the rise of Keynesian economic politics and also aroused sympathy for socialist and communist goals and strategies worldwide. The founders of neoliberal thinking realized that, due to the threat of socialism defeating capitalism, it wasn't possible to risk allowing the economic crisis of the 1930s to repeat, and therefore it was necessary to create an institutional framework that would check the excesses of an entirely unregulated market. Thus, it is possible to claim that neoliberalism acknowledged the meaning of the state primarily in order to prevent an economic crisis that would bring about the kinds of conditions that helped socialism and communism to spread, which would threaten the existence of capitalism.

Overall, we can state that neoliberalism carried out its capitalist revolution with the help of transformed elements that were bound to the diverse embodiments of the communist idea in the twentieth century. However, this was not a victory of neoliberalism over communism in the true sense, because the communist idea reached its internal limits and its effectiveness began to be extinguished by itself. Neoliberalism did not achieve victory over the communist idea but instead replaced it by refashioning some of its elements into a "new spirit of capitalism." The extinguishment of the communist idea and its replacement with this "new spirit of capitalism" manifested entirely empirically. Although productivity has grown since the 1970s, real wages have stagnated. In many graphs, we can see the growth of class inequalities to the point where it resembles the inequalities in the nineteenth and the beginning of the twentieth century—that is, before the beginning of the communist sequence in 1917.

Owning Yourself as Your Capital and the Mystery of the Neoliberal Subject (Foucault)

Thatcher, Klaus, and other neoliberal politicians promised that every citizen has the opportunity to become an owner of a certain form of capital, and I have termed this promise capitalized citizenship. However, neoliberalism doesn't understand capitalized citizenship only as property that a citizen owns (stocks, housing), but also as "human capital" that it identifies with the human being. In this context, it is necessary to focus on Foucault's analysis of neoliberalism, which became a starting point for many later theorists, among whom I will mention Wendy Brown, whose work we will discuss in the chapter on the present state of neoliberalism. Foucault captured the emergence of a neoliberal society that was abolishing the ideal of the disciplined society from the period of Fordian-Keynesian capitalism. Instead of a society based on orders, a society in the fundamental invisibility of the regulative processes was coming into existence. As Foucault noted, the invisibility of the hand of the market is crucial. The market works in such a way that no one is in control of its spontaneous oscillations and regulations, and it is precisely this invisibility and fundamental uncontrollability that—as Friedrich Hayek emphasized—disqualifies every political sovereign and every project for the collective good.[12] According to Foucault, a form of governance and of rationality is established that acts as a grid that shapes people's self-perception, forms of being, and also thinking. This grid is composed of economic patterns such as capital, investments, competency, and innovation, and these economic patterns are dispersed into all areas of human society, no matter how far removed they may seem from economic calculability. Foucault draws attention to the utopian element of neoliberalism, which is connected to what was discussed above about the transformations of and surrogates for communist elements.[13] Neoliberalism is not just a technology of government but a "general style of thought, analysis, and imagination," which, according to Hayek, is intended to create utopia-forming activities that give it the vitality and historical dynamism manifested by socialism. "Liberalism also needs utopia. It is up to us to create liberal utopias, to think in a liberal mode, rather than presenting liberalism as a technical alternative for government."[14] In my opinion, this utopianism, which Hayek explicitly associates with socialist utopianism, is linked to the belief that the invisible hand of the market is an anti-authoritarian mechanism that leads to overall social wealth. This belief is expressed in the idea of a "trickle-down" effect in which wealth will spontaneously flow from the wealthiest to a broader spectrum of social classes.

What neoliberal rationality has in common with escalating modernist politics is that, similar to Stalinism, it endeavors to transform the human being. This is done on the basis of market principles. Neoliberalism considers human beings to be active economic subjects with certain innate and acquired capital: their abilities, especially inventiveness, diligence, and hard work, and their acquired competencies. Capital is no longer an alienated social power as it had been for Marx because, in its basic meaning, it merges with the human being. There is an emancipatory element in neoliberalism: the idea that neoliberal labor does not create alienation, which according to Marx arises when, within the value-creating process, a certain portion of the labor force called surplus labor is alienated by the one who purchased this labor force for producing commodities—that is, the capitalist. Neoliberalism conceives of human capital in such a way that there is no alienation within it because abilities and competencies represent a capital that is the essential property of the individual. The laborer in neoliberalism becomes an individual who appears to him or herself as capital or as an enterprise of its kind. According to Foucault, a neoliberal society is made up of enterprise units that produce "machinery/flows" that increase their capital in the form of competencies. Depending on diverse variables, there will sooner or later be a corresponding increase in income. Neoliberalism changes the understanding of human activity in general, so we see that education, childrearing, medical care, and other previously non-economic activities begin to create human capital that will then generate income. This being the case, we should conceive of a wide range of human activities as investments into human capital. Foucault even noticed that neoliberalism leads to genetic programs that alter the genetic makeup of offspring with the aim of improving their human capital. Neoliberalism creates a need for eugenics that improve human capital.[15]

The human being as human capital raises the question of whether this form of self-conception, thought, and action creates a subject. In other words, does the human being become a subject in neoliberalism? Mitchell Dean argues that neoliberal regulations do not mean the internal "subjectivization" of individuals. Unlike other interpreters of Foucault's conception of neoliberalism, Dean is inclined to believe that Foucault doesn't actually understand human capital to be the result of subjectivizing mechanisms such as the identity of "opportunistic criminal" or "recidivist" known from disciplinary societies.[16] Foucault conceives of human capital in such a way that the human being becomes connected to neoliberal regulations in a manner different from the "production of subjectivity."

He argues that neoliberalism creates a space for a society in which "there is an optimization of systems of difference, in which the field is left open to fluctuating processes, in which minority individuals and practices are tolerated, in which action is brought to bear on the rules of the game rather than on the players, and finally in which there is an environmental type of intervention instead of the internal subjugation of individuals."[17] However, according to Dean's interpretation, this is not the case. The neoliberal subject is defined as self-investing human capital: one who is an enterprise unto him or herself. But this does not happen because the individual is the object of disciplinary practices that cause him or her to understand themselves in accordance with the identities produced by society, thereby acquiring their subjectivity, and thus their selves. Instead, neoliberalism creates a non-disciplinary type of regulation of human life that can inspire a feeling of liberation and satisfaction, because it leads away from a subjectivization that *directively* subordinates human individuality and makes the human being the object of classification, administration, and control.[18] Neoliberalism abolishes these disciplinary mechanisms, which created subjectivities that led to exclusion, such as the subjectivity of the "mentally disturbed person."

According to Foucault, neoliberalism brings about an optimization of the system of differences and tolerance for minority individuals and practices.[19] However, it does not sufficiently explain how the individual comes to identify with the neoliberal grid that shapes their being into the form of human capital. Or is this kind of identification not really taking place here? This problem concerns the question of how to understand neoliberal regulation without "subjectivization." According to Foucault, it is necessary to view neoliberalism primarily as a manner of operating or behaving (*manière de faire*), which pursues certain goals and regulates itself through constant reflection. In Foucault's conception of neoliberalism, therefore, the fact that neoliberalism represents a certain theory, ideology, or doctrine is not of crucial importance, nor is the fact that it creates a certain set of economic policies. Neoliberalism is a method of rationalizing the implementation of certain steps that follow the internal rules of the economy.[20]

Here, we arrive at a convoluted discussion of the character of neoliberal subjectivity as a result of a certain normativity. The question at stake is whether neoliberalism is similar to ideological systems that create norms which are then internalized as acts that can be described through concepts such as Foucault's subjectivization, Althusser's ideological interpellation, or the big Other in Lacan and Žižek. Are the methods of implementation that Foucault writes about norms that people adopt because they are legitimized through certain institutions (schools, universities, the media, politicians)? Lyotard writes that capitalism does not need to be legitimized and doesn't prescribe anything in the form of a strict obligation: it can do without the normative instance. It is not "totalitarian in a political sense," but on the other hand, it is because it "calls for the complete hegemony of the economic genre of discourse."[21] Every thing and every action is acceptable if it enters into neoliberal economic exchange, which must continually expand. Neoliberalism does not create any grand narrative or metanarrative as Marxism had. As Lyotard claims, neoliberalism is not affected by the disappearance of grand narratives, including the liberal narrative of the growth of wealth for all of humanity. Neoliberalism is compatible with all kinds of political regimes, including republicanism and despotism.[22] Lyotard's understanding of the matter is that capitalism is ubiquitous rather as a necessity than as a finality, even though he admits that a certain finality is hidden within neoliberal capitalism, which is "to save time." However, he leaves unanswered whether this finality is a parallel to the finality that operates in the universal narratives, or is merely a finality that is localized to specific places.

Foucault and Lyotard agree that neoliberalism is mainly a collection of economic approaches that aren't connected with a specific political doctrine or grand narrative. However, these thinkers are overlooking the political and ethical dimension of neoliberalism pointed out by Jessica Whyte, and they neglect the fact that neoliberalism fills in the empty space left behind by the embodiment of the communist idea. It was only its complete extinction that enabled the expansion of the "economic speech genre." The ubiquity of neoliberal capitalism and the appearance of its necessity is a result of the weakening and disappearance of the Marxist "metanarrative" that created political and state forms that restrained capital's global movements and cast doubt upon its necessity.

Neoliberalism's Emancipatory Promises

However, it's possible to agree with Foucault and Lyotard that people do not become human capital because they have internalized the neoliberal conception of the human being on the basis of an authoritative directive. Neoliberalism is not an ideology in the classical sense of the word, but it acts as a collection of practices relating to economic rationality that penetrate into every aspect of life. These practices and approaches do not have the nature of an order that obliges people to behave in certain ways. Neoliberalism does not proceed like Calvinist capitalism, which issued morally binding orders for diligence and modesty, as Max Weber described. If neoliberalism did this, it would have to create a new "grand narrative" as its source of legitimation that would be comparable to modern reformed Christianity, or to the Enlightenment or Marxism. Calvinist capitalism derived its moral commandments from the doctrine of predestination for salvation; a condition that displayed the worldly sign of wealth. However, neoliberalism doesn't arrive with a grand legitimizing story, as Foucault and Lyotard point out. Although it contains the ethical motives that Whyte writes about, as well as transmuted elements of emancipatory projects tied to the communist idea, these motifs and elements don't act as central concepts that would legitimize neoliberal practices in the way that the doctrine of salvation, which emphasized profit-seeking behavior, did in Calvinist capitalism. Neoliberal practices are not based on commands that would lead to performative acts of this type: "you have to be modest and hard-working in order to fulfill God's moral order." The non-commanding and non-disciplinary character of neoliberalism certainly made a liberating impression in the period when the social state was bureaucratizing and socialist countries appeared to be dictatorial regimes. In the period of the extinguishing and freezing of the communist idea, neoliberalism succeeded in adopting a transmuted form of the communist vision of a non-commanding and nonhierarchical society. Neoliberal thinkers and politicians have convinced a sufficient number of citizens that a non-commanding and nonauthoritarian society is actually possible, and that it's made by the free market.

However, the question remains of what is the basis of these neoliberal practices that regulate human society if neoliberalism isn't issuing directives and also generally refraining from disciplinary forms of subjectivization? Neoliberalism's egalitarian and general emancipatory promises are not fulfilled on the basis of political practices that compensate for losses suffered or actively regulate the market. Fulfilling these promises is outside of human control because the invisible hand of the market must remain invisible; that is, it cannot become the visible hand of certain specific economic policies or planning. So how is it possible to explain that citizens accept the neoliberal conception of the human being and behave like self-investing human capital?

Where does this principle of necessity inhere? No one issues orders that people should begin to behave like human capital, and yet they still recognize that this change has the character of necessity. Let us first consider the situation of the industrial laborer that Marx writes about. This laborer is free: no one orders him to sell his labor power, and thus work. Why did the free individual become an industrial laborer, and thus a capitalist subjectification has taken place in which he accepted the identity of a laborer? It is trivial to point out that he was forced into it by impersonal circumstances. If he had not begun to work and had not accepted a laborer's identity, he would experience serious existential consequences, such as physical suffering, cold, and hunger. We can term this reason for acquiring a certain identity *situational determination*. A person finds herself in a situation that forces her to adopt a certain identity, even without there being an authoritative order. It can be proven that in social and religious history, an authoritarian order was not only an act of subordinating another but also expressed a certain commitment to the person affected—at the very least, on a symbolic level. This minimal symbolic commitment appeared in all kinds of social and religious forms that can be summed up in the promise: "If you obey me, you'll enjoy my protection." Leaving aside the authoritarian violence associated with the initial accumulation of capital, which Marx had so vividly described on the basis of period documents, the initial field of decision-making in capitalism is precisely this non-directive situational determination. It evokes the impression of freedom to make decisions, and from the perspective of the liberal conception, the decisions are truly free, because individuals "voluntarily" express agreement with the sale of their labor power and confirm this agreement by signing an employment contract. This is non-directive determination, which has the nature of necessity. Its necessity consists in that if the "free individual" did not make a particular decision, they are going to face consequences that will ultimately affect their physical existence and perhaps also the existence of their loved ones.

People's connection to the neoliberal identity of human capital can be interpreted in a similar manner. One does not have to behave like human capital and can maintain a collective identity as a member of a trade union organizing a strike or as a conscious member of the working class. However, neoliberal politicians create a "free market" or recommodification of labor power through their deregulatory interventions (Offe), by which they establish situational determination. It consists of a discursive layer in which we find neoliberal ethical values and emancipatory promises, and a layer of unspoken existential circumstances. This existential layer brings about the need to adopt a neoliberal identity due to the consequences of not adopting it. These consequences affect human beings' living conditions and are often devastating: for example, long-term unemployment. Connecting with the identity of the human being as human capital is often motivated by a person lacking a chance to enter into full-value employment and therefore being forced to behave like an entrepreneur of their own being. Situational determination creates a specific relationship for human beings to themselves qua human capital. Although the neoliberal theory of human capital claims that human capital is not alienated from its bearer, it overlooks the motivation for people to take on this neoliberal identity in the first place. While the motivation may be neoliberal emancipatory promises, neoliberal politics at the same time creates economic conditions in which internalizing this identity becomes, as Spinoza would say, a recognized necessity. This nonauthoritative existential pressure means that the neoliberal identity of human capital remains fractured and inconsistent, as does the identity of the industrial laborer that Marx wrote about. This split may lie quietly for a long time without external manifestations of resistance, but it becomes apparent under certain conditions, as we saw with the mass protests against neoliberalism and global capital that erupted in full force in Europe and the United States in 2011 and 2012 (Occupy Wall Street, Indignados, the Czech "Stop vládě" movement, etc.). The neoliberal identity of human capital is not a coherent identity that expresses the continual process of the self's development, and in which it makes sense to speak of human autonomy and subjectivity. When one accepts the identity of human capital, it is not only an act of making a free decision by an individual, but it is also always the resulting effect of the action of external circumstances that can be understood as situational determination.

The neoliberal identity of human capital is not only fragmented in this way but it also has a paradoxical character if we attribute individualistic interest to it. Foucault defines "interest" after the models of classical liberal authors as an expression of non-transferable, atomistic choice that unconditionally relates to the subject him or herself.[23] But who is this subject in the case of neoliberal identity? Let us now pose the question of who or what this self is that is the bearer of human capital discussed above. Neoliberal emancipatory promises portray the citizen as the bearer of the right to self-ownership, which establishes his right to become his own enterprise. However, if we turn directly to the bearer of these rights (to their subject), we find that the individual exchanges their innate and acquired abilities for capital and begins to understand her entire being in this way, including her self. It's not at all clear what the bearer of human capital is when the human self has also changed into capital. If the classical definition of the subject is simple identity "I am I," from which human autonomy as well as the "non-transferable atomistic choice" are supposed to arise, after the transformation of the entire human being into capital, this formula (in the strict understanding) no longer applies. Here there is another formula that reads

"I am capital." It means that I shape my self in conformity with the neoliberal grid, so that economic categories such as investment, savings, competencies, innovations, and competition act upon me. I do not understand myself as a self that has a distance from the neoliberal grid that decides about its benefit to my interests from an autonomous position. So, if the self is deprived of this distance, how can it understand its autonomy? It is a self that does not ask what is in its *own* interest, but which defines its interest so that it corresponds to the neoliberal grid. Its interest is in prudently investing its abilities and in having its competencies rewarded by the market. It has free choice to determine where it will invest its capital, and it takes on the risk associated with this choice. However, in this way, it is acting precisely as human capital that shapes its "own choice" in conformity with this. The self identifies with neoliberal human capital, and thus loses its autonomous selfhood. It is ultimately for this reason, as Konrad Liessman points out, that the autonomous self, which continually develops its understanding of the world and of itself, is incompatible with the flexible values of neoliberal capitalism, which require the individual to be able and willing to swiftly change its competencies, knowledge, and way of seeing things.[24] As self-investing human capital, the human being shapes his self in accordance with the requirements for flexibility, variability, and fluidity. The human being is shaped according to market demands, and therefore lacks autonomy in the true sense of the word. A paradoxical conception of individual interest arises here, in which the individual is missing as an autonomous author of "non-transferable atomistic choice." It is an individualism without the individual, or egoism without an ego, which Adorno and Horkheimer wrote about using different terms in *Dialectic of Enlightenment*. The individuality of the individual, which characterizes her alone, has the form of a forced imitation in which the individual resembles a cultural commodity. Individuality means "hardly more than dazzling white teeth and freedom from body odor and emotions."[25] As early as the mid-1940s, Adorno and Horkheimer pointed to the helplessness and disintegration of individuality, which later made it possible to enforce the asubjective understanding of the human being as human capital.

This asubjective nature of human capital arises out of the fact that each type of capital expresses an exchange value. Although we can use capital to buy goods for our own use, its main purpose is exchange. Capital serves its own expanded reproduction (accumulation) through the mediation of relationships of exchange. When the human being functions as human capital, human qualities, abilities, and even genetic structure cease to have use value and become exchange value instead. These human qualities and abilities are not conceived of as evoking joy from creation or from learning, but are evaluated according to criteria of "success" or how well they have "proven themselves" in comparison with the abilities of others.[26] Individuality also becomes an exchange value. It is not a quality that expresses human subjectivity manifested by one's own judgments and unique appropriation of the world, but instead a quality whose value is measured by market valuation. Human capital does not relate to the individuality of the individual but is determined through exchange relations that are outside of the individual's control. Human capital therefore suppresses the individualism that is connected with the autonomy of the human subject. The neoliberal notion of individuality only means that the human being is individually responsible for her own enterprise, which is the exchange value of her human capital.

However, here the neoliberal promise of merit is operating, according to which the human being acting as human capital has to expect that the investments they made in their capital will sooner or later be adequately valued by the invisible hand of the market. This is a merit independent of the decisions of political authorities, because according to neoliberalism it arises spontaneously through the balancing of market forces. This principle of merit is ultimately fair, and it offers equal opportunities because each human being has a chance to raise the market valuation of their human capital on the basis of their abilities and their work. This market merit justice is portrayed as independent of the political authority that will decide it, and therefore it's a justice connected with the maximal possible freedom of the individual.

In the 1980s and 1990s, neoliberalism as a regulation of society without authoritative directives and direct disciplinary practices could have seemed like a liberation from the bureaucratic approaches of the social state and from political control of citizens under state socialism. However, its attractiveness was not only a negative distaste for continuing under a bureaucratic social state or in ossified forms of state socialism but it was also a positive attraction. Neoliberalism expressed emancipatory and egalitarian principles that gave rise to the impression that in neoliberalism citizens would have a new life, freed from bureaucratic domination and political supervision. It's no coincidence that since the 1930s, some Trotskyites in the United States have been inclined toward an emergent neoconservatism that combines the neoliberal criticism of the bureaucratic state with American conservative values.[27] In the Czech context, Rita Klímová, an economist and the wife of one of the main representatives of the Prague Spring, Zdeněk Mlynář, can serve as an example of the transition from communism to neoliberalism. As a dissident, she began attending housing seminars with neoliberal authors and gradually shifted over to a neoliberal position. In November 1989, she brought Václav Klaus into the emerging Civic Forum. These stories testify to former communists recognizing ideas and values in neoliberalism that had something in common with the ideals that once led them to commit to communism.

Neoliberalism's Core and Peripheral Patterns

In neoliberalism, there are two types of patterns during the first period of the interregnum. First, there are the formulas that are central to the neoliberal form of governance and rationality: the free market, spontaneous order, non-disciplinary regulation, privatization, competition, deregulation, limiting state expenditures, commodification, competencies, capital, human capital, and other categories associated with these. Let's term these core formulas. And then there are the patterns that relate to concepts and principles that have emerged in various embodiments of the communist idea in the twentieth century. These patterns were mostly created by the managerial and capitalist transmutation of emancipatory concepts and principles belonging to the communist idea, or they were created as a reaction to the threat to capitalism from states and movements that were committed to this idea in one way or another. Neoliberalism has made patterns out of them that became part of its own pattern, and they enhance the effectiveness of its core patterns. We can therefore term them peripheral or circulating patterns.

Peripheral neoliberal patterns that relate to communist elements are:

- A nonauthoritarian manner of governance that transforms the spirit of 1968 and strengthens one of the central neoliberal patterns, which is the non-disciplinary regulation of society associated with the market as a spontaneous order.
- The equality of capitalized citizenship, which assigns the ownership of capital—their own human capital—to all citizens.
- Merit, which creates a correlation between property and deservingness. Fresh ideas, diligence, hard work, and other abilities, competencies, and investments are rewarded by the market in such a way that sooner or later they lead to an increase in the value of human capital and bring adequate profit. Merit is connected with the harmonization and correlation functions of the invisible hand of the market.

- The role of the state in the form of administrative recommodification, in which state institutions, through privatization plans and corresponding laws, oversee the regulated transfer of property into the free market. State institutions ensure the conditions for the further development of the free market.

These peripheral and neoliberal patterns do not have the same character and origin, and therefore are not entirely mutually coherent. The spirit of 1968, which was transformed into nonauthoritarian managerial practices, is in a certain tension with the principle of state institutions that make political decisions about steps that should create and maintain conditions for the development of the free market. I have written above that this etatist element of neoliberalism was created negatively as insurance against an economic crisis that would strengthen states and movements that sought to overcome capitalism. Although these patterns are peripheral in neoliberalism, in the 1970s and 1980s during the period of the extinction of the communist idea, they significantly helped establish neoliberalism as a specific form of governance and rationality. As these peripheral patterns begin to weaken and disappear, the character of the core patterns changes. They cease to display their original effectiveness and vitality. These peripheral patterns can therefore be considered as having a prosthetic nature. They create certain prostheses without which the free market, deregulation, competition, human capital, and other core principles of neoliberalism begin to produce unintended effects and to fracture from within. The period begins in which neoliberalism comes into crisis. The first period of neoliberalism lasted roughly from the beginning of the 1980s until the financial crisis of 2008, with the year 1989 symbolizing its worldwide triumph, but also the beginning of its difficulties. The financial crisis also marks the beginning of the second period of neoliberalism, which already also belongs to the present period of interregnum. We will discuss this in the next part of the book.

2

Postmodernism, in Which Modernism Is Extinguished

Postmodernism as a Transitional Culture

The interregnum is also manifested in culture, which I conceive of as a complex structure of certain patterns (cultural patterns), which appear with various modifications as the dominant signs of human thinking (cognitive forms), experience ("structures of experience"), and expressions (manners of acting and of ethical decision-making). I am basing this on a structurally analytical approach that has been used in the works of many cultural and social theorists, such as Raymond Williams, Pierre Macherey, Ihab Hassan, Fredric Jameson, and Slavoj Žižek. Art and theory are thus a part of culture, but they are not everything that makes up culture. In modern philosophy, Hegel's concept of the "epochal state of spirit" is an analogous concept, and another one in historiography would be the concept of "mentality" that was elaborated by the Annales school. The culture that arrives at the end of the 1960s is postmodernism. Why can postmodernism be considered the culture that belongs to the interregnum?

Postmodernism corresponds to the definition of the interregnum as a period in which the truth procedures connected to the communist idea were closed, as was art in the modernist project. Postmodernism is also understood as a transitional period by Jameson, who has defined it as a period between the two stages of capitalism, as we have seen in the Introduction. Postmodernism contains a position within itself that Jacques Derrida expressed as "the work of mourning." In the eulogy he delivered at Louis Althusser's grave, he summed up this position by saying it is not only this or that thing that is leaving with Althusser, but that a world itself, or a "source of a world" in which we experienced an irreplaceable story which was disappearing irretrievably with him.[1] In this melancholy, one can see a sign that postmodernism arises in the period of the end of the world whose source was truth procedures. According to Lyotard, postmodernism does not begin with the discovery of a clearly defined new style that would negate the previous style, but instead declares itself as a feeling of fatigue with modernism's emptiness, and a lack of faith in its "grand narratives."[2] In this statement by Lyotard, it's possible to decipher a message about the extinction of truth procedures, which tells us that postmodernism arises in the period when they end. From this perspective, it's not controversial to claim that we can understand postmodernism as a culture that belongs to the interregnum, which we define as the period after the closing of truth procedures.

The period of the extinction of artistic and political truth procedures brought about a similar effect in culture, which we have encountered in neoliberalism. The core patterns of postmodernism are connected with modernist patterns, which make up their peripheral shadow supplements and "contaminate" the typology of postmodernism.

Shadow Modernism

Jameson, Speaks, Huyssen, Anderson, Toth, and other cultural theorists have noted that postmodernism didn't have a pure form when it arose, and it was actually never pure. Jameson conceives of this phenomenon as meaning that residual traces of modernism are necessary failures caused by the fact that postmodernism is additionally related to the coordinates of modernism, which begin to manifest in a new way.[3] Andreas Huyssen argues that while the early postmodernism of the 1970s radically criticized modernism, its revolt against institutionalized modernism manifested like the last stage of the avant-garde. There is no fundamental break that separates postmodernism and modernism.[4] And if there is no such break, and postmodernism contains residual traces of modernism, the relationship between postmodern patterns and modernist patterns changes. In his typology of postmodernism and modernism, Ihab Hassan set these patterns into opposition, so, for example, the postmodern "dispersal" is the opposite of the modernist "concentration," and the postmodern "fragment" is the opposite of the modernist "whole."[5] However, according to the thesis of the impurity of postmodernism, these two types of patterns are not in opposition. Along with the postmodern "dispersal" or "fragment," the "concentration" and the "whole" also emerge in shadow form. Postmodernist patterns are never purged of their modernist counterparts in philosophy, art, or social practices, so, for example, the "dispersal" that we find in Derrida's concepts of dissemination and deconstruction also evokes a weak form of "concentration," as we see in Derrida's idea of absolute justice or "minimal ideality" as the "undeconstructable condition of deconstruction."[6] Derrida's concept of the "trace" expresses the impossibility of reaching a complete and unambiguous meaning of words as representations of our perception or of external reality, but at the same time, it enables the existence of the concept of meaning and representation. The same is also true of Derrida's neologism *différance*, which expresses the impossibility of the full presence of meaning, but creates the possibility of a distinction between presence and absence, which maintains a "metaphysical" longing for presence. *Différance* thus evokes that which it makes impossible. As Josh Toth has noted, Derrida never completely separated himself from the project of modernism, as it was expressed in phenomenology and structuralism. His returns to ontotheology, logocentrism, and humanism are not accidental slips.[7]

The Spectral Existence of Modernism in Postmodernism (Toth and Derrida)

Josh Toth uses Derrida's notion of the specter from the latter's book *Specters of Marx* and developed a "spectroanalysis" to express the manner in which remnants of modernism are present in postmodern texts. His method consists in a doubled reflection in which he changes the doubled reflection, in which Derrida's given concept, which is itself a reflection of the presence of a modernist "specter" (the presence of meaning, unity, absolute justice, political messianism), into a metareflection of Derrida's conception and postmodern philosophy as a whole. Toth understands the presence of modernism in postmodernism in such a way that modernist "specters" are hidden in the underground of modernism, and emerge from there into postmodernists texts as soon as the author attempts to definitively banish them from the underground and create a pure postmodernism. Toth interprets these returns of modernism as a motivation to the further advancement of postmodernism, which is supposed to save us from the underground specters. As he writes, Derrida's repeated efforts to separate deconstruction, and in particular its concepts of *différance*, the "trace," and "supplementarity" from all the remnants of modernism and ontotheological discourse is a symptom of his hostility toward the specters, his frightened hostility, which sometimes resists this terror with an explosion of laughter. In Toth's view, the early stages of Derrida's deconstruction can be defined in the same way the late Derrida conceives of Marxism—as a discourse that is terrified of specters while at the same time being dependent on them.[8]

From this point of view, I understand the late Derrida's turn to undeconstructable conditions as a consequence of his awareness that his texts contain an unconscious level where modernist and communist specters appear. I understand Derrida's introduction of Marx's ghost to the scene in the form of a concept of absolute justice toward the unique as an attempt at domesticating it within the house of deconstruction. This spirit then no longer appears as an unpredictable phantom from the underworld, but is instead clothed in garments woven from deconstruction. In this point, I do not entirely agree with Toth's analysis of spectrality in postmodernism. The domestication of this specter does not take place until Derrida's late career. Toth's claim that for Derrida modernism is a specter of the same type as the horizon of communism is for liberal democracy is true for his early career, but not for the late Derrida who wrote *Specters of Marx*. Derrida consciously includes this specter in his text as a certain constitutive condition of deconstruction, whereas liberal democracy does not consciously do any such thing. For liberal democracy, communism remains a mere specter whose return is to be prevented.

Toth also discovers a ghostly presence of modernism in Lyotard's conception of paralogy. He points out that we find both a radically emancipatory element and also a trace of the avant-garde imperative to "novelty" and "experiment." Lyotard's heterogeneous speech games draw their legitimacy from a practice that creates instability and undermines the unifying framework that regulated knowledge. I see this form of practice as a trace of the communist idea that was shaped in the events of May 1968. Paralogous practice enables the arrival of the radically new, and offers space for experiments, because thanks to it the production of knowledge, and experimentation are not bound to the unifying truths of a metanarrative. Lyotard therefore claims that postmodern paralogy is an extreme form of experiment and avant-garde production of the new.[9] Toth sees in Lyotard's conception of postmodernism an "ironic return" to the metanarrative of emancipation, because Lyotard believes that humanity, which himself understands as a heterogeneous mass of discursively determined nodal points, is seeking emancipation through the practice of paralogy. The modernist emancipatory project therefore remains, in Toth's view, a reviving moment in postmodernism, even though the denial of this project is its defining trait. This emancipatory project is a specter that "returns through its denial, or because of, its denial."[10]

Even though Toth's explanation is revealing and also surprising to many, spectrality here de facto only appears here as a Derridean metaphor that expresses the conceptual figure of the "return of the repressed" that was previously introduced by Freud and philosophically and sociologically adapted by Adorno and Horkheimer. However, Toth's interpretation of the spectral presence of modernism doesn't exhaust the ways in which modernism exists in postmodernism. An example is Deleuze's reterritorialization, which Deleuze and Guattari understand as a production that takes place along with the production of deterritorialization. In Deleuze's conception reterritorialization cannot be conveniently interpreted as a return of the repressed, even though it is also possible to conceive of it in this way from a certain perspective. It is certainly also the return of a weakened definition that appears in a stronger form in modernism; however, it is not a return of the repressed in the sense Toth speaks about. Deleuze conceives of reterritorialization as a production that does not take place in the underground production of deterritorialization because it is not displaced by this kind of production. Rather, there is a co-production of two modes of vital flow that are mutually intertwined (reterritorialization is never separated from deterritorialization), and no displacement occurs. In reality, Deleuze's postmodernism has nowhere to return to as a specter, because the elements of modernism are transformed directly on the philosophical scene.

The case is similar with Hardt and Negri's concept of the multitude, which is inspired by Deleuze. These authors point even more strongly than Deleuze and Guattari to the connection between postmodernist patterns (dispersal, radical plurality, and diversity) and the weakened modernist patterns (concentration and unification). Hardt and Negri do not see the scattering or disintegration of social organizations and communities as the only tendency asserted in neoliberal and post-Fordist capitalism. Along with this dispersal, a "multitude" is created as a shared tissue that contains countless internal differences (cultural, ethnic, gender, class) within it while at the same time also containing something that is shared among all. On the one hand there is a "swarm intelligence" that corresponds to Marx's "general intellect," and on the other there is its biopolitical production that creates a commons.[11] Hardt and Negri's conception of the multitude contains radically emancipatory and utopian elements connected with a euphoric impulse. These elements of the multitude are not the return of a specter, but are instead the production of a new type of social substance that in the eyes of these authors transcends the unifying modernism, but without ending up with a one-dimensional emphasis on singularity.

Postmodernist Euphoria and Its Transformation

In Hardt and Negri, a euphoric position of thought appears, evoked by the conscious possibility that the tendency to create a multitude as a non-unifying tissue of common social being will continue to grow stronger—although it is impossible to know in advance when it will happen. However, this euphoric position is possible to understand as a manifestation of the affectivity that appears in postmodern philosophy, art, and cultural in general. It is an affectivity that is not ubiquitous in postmodernism: we mainly find it in the early phase. Huyssen describes how in the 1970s postmodern artists and theorists shared a euphoric vision of a post-industrial society and professed techno-optimism. The postmodern cultural theorist Ihab Hassan praised "runaway technology," the "boundless dispersal by media," and "the computer as substitute consciousness."[12] Jameson also writes about this techno-optimism, claiming that the modernist euphoria from the new was prolonged in early postmodernism, manifesting in the postmodernist enchantment with high-tech information technology.[13] As Huyssen writes, these euphoric visions were associated with the "populist" trend of postmodernism that counterposed pop music, rock, popular literature, and various aspects of everyday life to institutionalized modernist art.[14] Postmodernism subverted the conservative and anticommunist politics of art during the period of the Cold War, and followed in the footsteps of dadaism, futurism, and other early avant-garde trends. However, postmodernist euphoria was not limited to technological euphoria. Its euphoria was also aroused by the belief that postmodernist revolt and subversive practices have something in common with protest stances in the popular classes.

In this way we can explain the postmodernist euphoria and its changes: in early postmodernism there was a technological and political euphoria that energized postmodernist concepts and approaches. Dispersal, deconstruction, rhizomatic models, indetermination, polymorphy, and performativity acted as a vital and subversive element that undermined and dissolved the ossified hierarchical structures that dominated artistic operations and social life.

This euphoria testifies to the fact that the truth procedures of modernist and avant-garde art, as well as the truth procedures connected with the communist idea, are burning out in early postmodernism. Early postmodernism only changes, so to speak, the text that is inscribed in them. It inscribes elements into it that have operated to subvert the forms that were sometimes used as tools for the suppression of these procedures in the twentieth century (the state, organizations, discipline, or the productive subject). The pouring of the subversive element into the cooling traces after the previous embodiments of modernist and communist procedures brings about a special effect of short-term reignition of these traces with a material that was not originally present in them. For example, one of these traces is a critical distance from capitalism. After the collapse of the communist truth procedure this trace cools off, because it is disconnected from truth procedures and their force of attraction. Early postmodernism filled this cooling trace with its subversive element, which in this case concerned the subversion of stable structures with centrally regulated binary differences. The result is a temporary reignition. The postmodern element, which focuses on the subversion of stable structures, was fused with the cooling trace that expresses "critical distance from capitalism" and a copulative relationship arose in the form of "subversion of stable structures is a criticism of capitalism." The notion of a "critical distance from capitalism," which lost its semantic meaning, came back to life thanks to its fulfillment of the modern element. However, its postmodern significance is separated from other traces that the truth procedure and its embodiments had left behind. There is no connection with the idea and practice of the political organization of resistance or of socioeconomic analysis of capitalism, unless what we mean by this is Deleuze and Guattari's books *Anti-Oedipus* and *A Thousand Plateaus*, where they examine the psychoanalytical and ontological effects of modern capitalism. Due to this isolation from other evental traces of modernism and communism, postmodern subversion connects up with the given trace (the concept of "a critical distance from capitalism") only temporarily. This subversive material, which ignites the event trail of truth, burns out, and the trace is also extinguished. Postmodernist subversion is separated from the concept of "a critical distance from capitalism," but its practice is energetically pumped up for a certain time from its encounter with the evental trace of the truth. This experience remains unconscious in postmodern practices, as Josh Toth would express it.

According to Huyssen, this euphoria abandoned postmodern artists and theorists in the mid-1970s, when the iconoclasm and subversiveness or pop, rock, and the sexual revolution was exhausted and these became cultural goods that were incorporated into capitalist circulation. Techno-optimism was replaced by a sober to critical reaction to mass media, which were acting more and more as instruments of commercial communications. The gloomy prognoses of the Club of Rome, which predicted serious threats to human civilization as a result of unlimited growth that disrupted the planetary ecological system also had their effect.[15] To these factors, we can also add the retreat of experimental political activities that continued the spirit of 1968 that were discussed above. The postmodern euphoria disappears during the period of the extinction of the communist idea. We can interpret the ironic distance from "grand narratives" that has typified postmodern art and philosophy since the 1970s as a defensive reaction to the loss of euphoria that came from the act of denying the previous state of euphoria.

As Toth and Huyssen claim, postmodernism abandoned its avant-garde inspirations in the late 1970s and in the 1980s, and it split into two currents. The first emerged as a conformist eclectic culture without any sign of criticism of the system, and the second partially retained its nonconformism, expressing critical perspectives on the status quo: this one attempted to purge itself of the remnants of "essentialism" that had penetrated it from the avant-garde and modernism.[16]

We can grasp the politicization of postmodernism that we can see in the late Derrida, particularly in the book *Specters of Marx*, as overcoming ironization as a defensive reaction to the blocked euphoria in the 1970s that had been caused by the extinction of the trace of the communist idea. Derrida evokes Marx's spirit or spirits that, for him, symbolize communism as a "messianism without a Messiah," an ideal of absolute justice toward the singular. This idea expresses the condition of the possibility of deconstruction that is also a condition of impossibility. Once this communist idea begins to materialize in real history, the principle of absolute justice toward the singular would be violated and thereby the condition of deconstruction would disintegrate. In other words, deconstruction relates to the absolute justice of communism as its condition, under the assumption that communism will have the form of a spirit or specter that does not materialize in history.

Derrida is not ironic toward Marx's spirit as such if we consider that he implored it not to leave, and he attributes to it a constitutive role in the movement of deconstruction. We can understand this turn by Derrida as an act of making the trace visible that Marx's politically materialized spirit had left in 1968. His traces were obscured or entirely airbrushed out in the 1970s in the eclectic and conformist current of postmodernism and in the critical current of postmodernism they were silent witnesses to the postmodern "childish" euphoria. They were witnesses who were meant to be forgotten. The late Derrida let these witnesses speak, and thus performed an anamnesis of the beginnings of modernism. However, this does not restore the postmodernist euphoria, nor does Derrida even seek to do so. In this anamnesis, melancholy develops as an experience of the impossibility of a return of euphoria, and Derrida expresses through the expression "the work of mourning" in a book with the eponymous title.

Postmodernism's Core and Peripheral Patterns

Jameson, Hassan, and other cultural theorists have formulated a number of patterns that appear in all kinds of modifications in postmodern theoretical and art texts, in the fine arts, film, political culture, intellectual life, and in interpersonal relationships. As stated in the Introduction, postmodernism is a culture that lost its sense for generalizing, and therefore it whispers to theorists, art critics, and artists that the very use of these generalizing patterns of problematic, because it's necessary to primarily focus on specific art objects, life stories, and social situations. Jameson terms this *generally* shared departure from everything general "postmodern nominalism." The use of these formulas thus gives rise to a minimal distance from the phenomena that fill the labyrinth of the contemporary world—a distance that is necessary so we can create coordinates that allow us to orient ourselves within the labyrinth.

Cultural theorists had already discovered the existence of patterns that operate within postmodernism the 1970s. If we stand at even a slight distance from the "blooming, buzzing confusion of immediate reality" (Jameson), we easily recognize that a similar way of thinking and experiencing things, as well as similar approaches have appeared in various genres. It is perhaps trivial to say that deconstruction is used, or has been used, as a certain approach or movement not only in philosophy, but also in theater and opera productions, video installations, novels, texts of literary criticism, historical and sociological research, and political speeches. In various corners of cultural life we find many further approaches, reactions, and expressive means that are generally shared. Let us at least name some of the patterns formulated by Jameson, Hassan, and other cultural theorists: multiplicity, difference, radical plurality, the dispersal of a pregiven meaning, random combinations of motifs, preference for idiolects (i.e., creating unique language creations without regard for language norms), indeterminate forms, hybrid styles, logical discontinuity, and schizoid styles of thought and speech, superficiality and spaciousness, heterogeneity, and uniqueness. These, as well as other patterns, are considered to characterize postmodern culture, and therefore there's nothing controversial in calling them core formulas. Just as we can recognize the Baroque, Mannerism, the

Renaissance, and Gothic styles according to certain traits, even though the lines are sometimes blurred or there is some ambiguity we can also recognize postmodernism according to certain traits, because core patterns are simply the identifying signs of the given culture.

Jameson, Toth, Huyssen, and other cultural theorists have discovered that these core traits are never pure, because they are connected in various ways with modernist patterns. As we have seen above, "dispersal," in the forms of Derrida's dissemination and deconstruction evokes a weak form of concentration, which is the idea of absolute justice as the condition for the possibility and the impossibility of deconstruction. Lyotard's conception of radical plurality in the form of paralogy brings about an "ironic return" of the metanarrative of emancipation and offers space to the modernist conception of "novelty." Deleuze and Guattari write that the movement of deterritorialization, which sets boundaries into indeterminate movement, produces a movement of reterritorialization in which a non-essential transitional boundary is established. Hardt and Negri's conception of the "multitude" as a tissue-like social formation with countless internal differences creates a "commons" and expresses radically emancipatory visions. in the case of the multitude, it can be assumed that its radically emancipatory vision has a more intensive existence here than in the other cases, and therefore it is a borderline formation that we can associate with phenomena that appear in the second period of the interregnum, which was discussed earlier. In the history of postmodernism, then avant-garde impulses appear, as do techno-optimism and euphoria, which then transform, disappear into the unconsciousness of text, and then reemerge in a different form.

"Concentration," "novelty," "euphoria," "techno-optimism," "emancipation," "subversion," and "critique" represent modernist patterns that are applied in postmodernism. They are not its defining features; they operate more around the margins and sometimes even in an invisible or unconscious manner, if we leave aside the borderline case of Hardt and Negri's "multitude." I therefore call this composition, which is analogous to the composition of neoliberalism, peripheral.

Postmodernism as Epicyclical Circulation

Timotheus Vermeulen and Robin van den Akker, in their conception of metamodernism, which I will deal with in detail in the next part of the book, created a model that captures the oscillation between postmodernist and modernist patterns. Metamodernism is one of the names for the culture that comes after postmodernism, in which both postmodernism and modernism have attractive force. I am bringing up these authors at this point is in order to introduce readers to the approach that helped me arrive at a model of the formations that captures the distribution and movements of these two types of patterns in postmodernism and in contemporary culture. Vermeulen and van den Akker's model of culture after the end of postmodernism illustrates oscillation between the postmodern and the modern fields. I explain this in more detail in the subchapter "A general model of contemporary culture: metamodernism" in the section dedicated to the present phase of the interregnum. In the following subchapter, "Deficiencies of the Metamodernist Model" I acquaint readers with the reasons why I do not consider this model altogether satisfactory, and why I transform it into a geometric shape. First, it was necessary to reach the end of the interpretation of contemporary culture; that is, at the end of the second section on the present interregnum, in order to develop a model of present culture and the present period of the interregnum on the basis of Vermeulen's and van den Akker's portrayal of metamodernism. As I explain in the appropriate place, Vermeulen and van den Akker's portrayal of metamodernism was based on certain ideas about postmodernism that turned out to be problematic. These authors did not pay enough attention to the fact that circulations similar to those within metamodernism are already found in postmodernism. Readers will only fully understand why I have suggested an epicycloid and ellipse as cultural models after they have become better acquainted with Vermeulen and van den Akker's portrayal of metamodernism and consider my reservations about it. To better understand the geometric modeling of postmodernism that follows, I recommend skipping over the part of the book that deals with individual phenomena of the present interregnum and first becoming acquainted with the issue of modeling culture in the subchapters devoted to this topic.

As I have demonstrated above, there are various ways that modernism exists within postmodernism. There is not only the "spectral" presence that Toth writes about, but also presence in the form of production (Deleuze, Hardt and Negri), and in the form of displaced affect in the case of euphoria.

If we create a model of the relationship between postmodernism and modernism in the first period of the interregnum, we cannot take these modes of modernism's existence into account because of the necessary simplification. Our goal will be to show the individual procedures, conceptions, and general formations created by Derrida, Lyotard, Deleuze, and others (deconstruction, paralogy, deterritorialization) in their relations to both pattern types. In the examples provided, we have seen circulations around postmodernist patterns (diffusion, radical plurality, disruption of boundaries, irony) and modernist patterns (concentration, novelty, setting boundaries, euphoria). We already know that postmodernist patterns are at the core and modernist patterns are peripheral. Modernist patterns have maintained a certain gravitational field around themselves, but they are much weaker than the gravitational field of postmodernist patterns. In postmodern philosophy, just like in postmodern art, there are circulations that cannot be represented as circulations around two poles with the same force of gravitation because they are peculiar eccentric circulations whose central points are made up of the core patterns. Is there any formation that has this feature? If we search through the repertoire of geometric shapes, we do find one that meets this criterion: the *epicycloid*. It is created when we take a circle with a center, and a second circle is rotating around its circumference. The external circle rotates around the circumference of the inner circle in such a way that the line that expresses its diameter during this rotation creates a curve whose furthest point from the inner circle equals the diameter of the outer circle. At some points, this curve intersects with the diameter of the inner circle. This type of rotation of the outer circle is called rolling, and it creates the representation the epicycloid (Figure 1).

The epicycloid represents a circulation that illustrates the movement around postmodernist and modernist patterns that take place within postmodernism as the culture of the first period of the interregnum. The center of the inner circle (*P*) represents the postmodernist core patterns, while the center of the circle, which rotates around the inner circle (*M*), expresses modernist peripheral patterns. On the circumference of the epicycloid are individual formations that arise in the first period of the interregnum ($F_{1,} F_{2,\ldots,} F_{n}$) in positions at various distances from *P*.

When representing a specific formation (F), we place the appropriate postmodern pattern into the inner circle and put the corresponding modernist pattern in the center of the peripheral circle. In the case of Derrida's approach to deconstruction, the "dispersal" pattern is in the *P* position, and the "concentration" pattern is in the *M* position. In Lyotard's concept of paralogy, we put "radical plurality" in position *P* and "novelty" or "unity" in position *M*. And we proceed in the same way with all the other formations of the first period of the interregnum. The patterns of dispersal, disrupting boundaries, irony, and indetermination go into the *P* position in the center of the inner circle, while the patterns of concentration, setting boundaries, euphoria, determination, and so

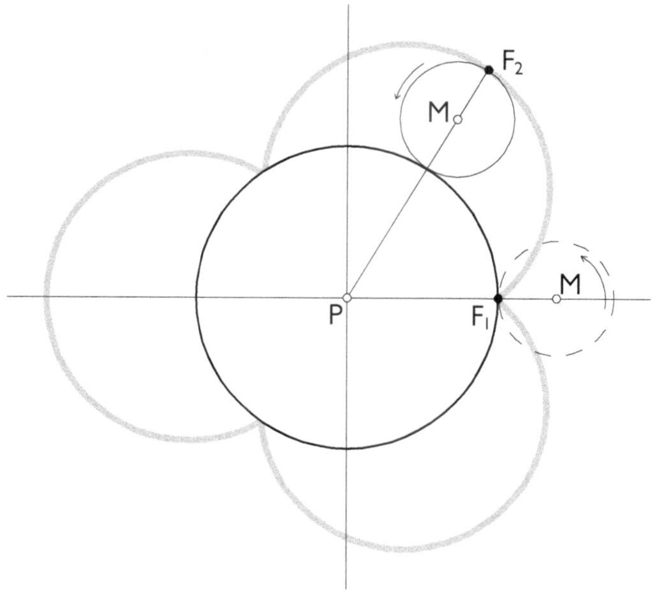

Figure 1 The epicycloid as a model of postmodernism (the first period of the interregnum) © Michael Hauser.

on, belong in the *M* position in the center of the peripheral circle. These patterns either alternate in the position or they coexist, depending on the type of analysis selected. In postmodern philosophy and art, we can focus on one pattern and its various modifications and transformations, or on a "cluster" of these patterns.

The epicycloid captures the circulation around the postmodernist and modernist patterns. By circulation, I mean the thought or creative movement of production, through which a particular approach, conception, or—more generally—formation of postmodern philosophy or postmodern art emerges in one author or another. Circulation is a representation of this production, which in specific cases does not conform to these patterns as predetermined "ideal types," but moves in their gravitational fields and creates various modifications of them that are ideal. The formula of "radical plurality" takes on the specific form of Lyotard's "paralogy," Derrida's "*différance*," or Hardt and Negri's "internal differentiation in the multitude," according to the given way of thinking and the internal relationships of their philosophy.

As a model, the epicycloid also expresses another property of the formations that arise in the circulations around the postmodernist and modernist patterns, whose force of attraction or gravitational fields differ. The stronger force of attraction, or a stronger gravitational field of postmodernist patterns in relation to those of modernist patterns, is represented in the size difference between the inner circle and the outer one. The approach to modernist formulas is based on the approach to postmodernist formulas, with the range of movement of the external circle depending on the size of the internal circle. The curve of the outer circle's movement depends on the inner circle of postmodernist patterns, so that its range is determined by the size of the inner circle. The larger the "postmodernist" circle is, that is, the bigger its gravitational field is, the greater the peripheral circle's projection into the inner circle will be, and the smaller the gravitational pole of the modernist patterns. The epicycloid model even makes it possible to represent a situation where the action of the modernist patterns is so weak that these patterns cease to influence the resulting form of the overall production, even though they still remain present. In the epicycloid model, we illustrate this situation by moving the center of the outer circle to the perimeter of the inner circle, and the resulting shape of the circulation is a simple circle, as shown by the position of point U_1. This is the situation we already encountered with Derrida, who at some point made the modernist element expressed as absolute justice or Marx's specter invisible during a certain period. As Toth has shown, this element was present in the "underground" of his philosophy. The shape of Derrida's symbolic production in this period is represented by the epicycloid in the form of a circle with inconspicuous deviations. In the late period, this element became visible as the theme of the book *Specters of Marx*. At that time, the shape of the epicycloid changed, and its shape of the circle took on a distinctive eccentric curve on the perimeter. Derrida's conceptions from the book *Specters of Marx* correspond to the position of point U_2. The same is true of the patterns of irony and euphoria. In early postmodernism, the euphoria is so strong that in the epicycloid model its circle is the same size as the inner circle of irony. As an element of cultural production, euphoria occupies the position of point U_2. In the next period the euphoria becomes invisible and the entire formation resolves into the shape of a circle. The cultural production has the position F_1. In the following period, the euphoria returns, for example, in the form of the euphoria connected with the radical emancipatory vision of Hardt and Negri's multitude. In this case, the epicycloid changes shape from a circle into its eccentric form. The epicycloid enables the representation of the intensity of the effect or, metaphorically speaking, the size of the gravitational field of individual patterns. It is a model that can be shaped diachronically so that it will change according to how the intensity of the action of the patterns analyzed have changed over time. It captures the dynamic course of changes in the positions and intensities of individual formulas. It is precisely these characteristics of the epicycloid that lead me to the conclusion that it would be difficult to find a more apt model to illustrate the transformations of cultural formations in the first period of the interregnum in relation to the postmodernist and modernist patterns.

Conclusion of the FIRST Section One

The Epicyclic Character of the First Period of the Interregnum

The epicycloid is a model that captures the arrangement of patterns in postmodernism, such as the "impure" or "mixed" transition culture of the first period of the interregnum. Can we also use it to organize the patterns in neoliberalism? I see no reason not to do so if we have also identified the core and peripheral patterns in neoliberalism. As was already stated, neoliberalism is a specific discourse and form of governance and rationality whose core or defining formula consists of the free market, spontaneous order, non-disciplinary regulation, privatization, competition, deregulation, restraint in government expenditures, commodification, competencies, capital, human capital, and other related categories. In addition to these patterns, we have also discovered peripheral patterns in it that relate in their various modifications to the traces of communist elements. These are their formulas: a nonauthoritarian style of management, the equality of capitalized citizenship, merit, and anti-crisis measures taken by the state. We can interpret the relationship between the core and peripheral patterns of neoliberalism using the model of the epicycloid. Consider, for example, the relationship between the peripheral pattern of "equality of capitalized citizenship" and the core pattern of "capital": the principle of equality has changed in the intensity of its action. In Václav Klaus's neoliberal politics, it manifested in the creation of the "coupon privatization" program that offered the promise to every citizen that they would own a certain form of stock capital. In the epicycloid model, the size of the rotating circle has grown, and an epicycloid appears with a strongly curved perimeter. In a period when there is a "tunneling" of companies as the culmination of the coupon privatization, whose only real requirement was to transfer state property into private capital as quickly as possible, the shape of the epicycloid changes. The center of the peripheral circle, which symbolizes the formula "equality of capitalized citizenship," falls onto the circumference of the circle defined by the formula of "capital." This principle of equality has a zero degree of intensity. It's necessary to add here that the peripheral patterns of neoliberalism were effectual thanks to their relationship to the traces of communist elements that were still operating with a fair degree of intensity in the 1970s and 1980s. For the sake of simplification, I do not include these traces of communist elements in the model of the neoliberal epicycloid. However, their degree of intensity influences the character of the peripheral patterns. As an example, let's take the peripheral formula of "anti-crisis state measures." As soon as the danger that the economic crisis will lend strength to anti-capitalist movements and increase the chance that socialist countries will defeat capitalism fades away, anti-crisis state measures weaken. This pattern falls down to the circumference of the inner circle, which is defined by the core pattern of the "free market." The weakening of the anti-crisis state measures that led to the financial crisis in 2008 can be represented as a diminishment or complete disappearance of epicyclic deviations on the circumference of the inner circle of neoliberalism. We can represent the financial crisis of 2008 as an epicycloid in the shape of a circle. We could also make a "cluster" of the core patterns, which we place into the center of the inner circle, as well as combining the peripheral patterns into the "cluster" and placing them into the center of the outer circle. By using the epicycloid model, we can approach neoliberalism in a new way and analyze it from three perspectives. The first is the "cluster" or the network of relationships within the core patterns; that is, the connection between the free market, spontaneous order, non-disciplinary regulation, and so on. The second is that we will connect the peripheral patterns and study the relationship between the nonauthoritarian style of management, the equality of capitalized citizenship, merit, and anti-crisis state measures. The third perspective combines the two previous ones and means that we will insert these two networks of patterns into the position of the core and periphery in the epicycloid model. By doing so, we get a complex, dynamic, and internally articulated image of neoliberalism, which can be elaborated as the subject of another book.

However, the most remarkable phenomenon is the structural similarity of neoliberalism and postmodernism that we discover by using the epicycloid model. The outer circle of the epicycloid captures the presence of patterns that act as deviations from specific prevailing tendencies within the areas of economics and culture. At the same time, these "disruptive" patterns are not heterogeneous and disconnected from specific models of neoliberalism and postmodernism. In the places where they shape specific economic or cultural movements, for example, the egalitarian elements of privatization or the euphoric position of postmodernism, they are still in interrelationship with the patterns that define neoliberalism or postmodernism. This fact is expressed by the dependence of the curve of overall circulation on both circles, which, however, are not in the same position, because one is core and the other is peripheral. In economics and culture, we have noted the effect of communist truth procedures, and in the second case, also of the effect of the modernist procedure, with both of these procedures being in a state of undergoing extinction. Their effect on neoliberalism and postmodernism had various modifications that we have examined with individual patterns.

In general, it can be argued that the fading presence of the above-mentioned procedures was of crucial importance for the very existence of the "disruptive" patterns within neoliberalism and postmodernism. The action of the "disruptive" patterns weakens to the extent that the traces of communist or modernist truth procedures are weakening. These "disruptive" patterns relate in various ways to the traces of truth procedures (a relationship of delimitation, spectrality, or negation), even though it was precisely these "disruptive" procedures that enabled neoliberalism and postmodernism to assert themselves socially (see the egalitarianism of the coupon privatization or the euphoria of early postmodernism). Neoliberalism and postmodernism are thus dependent in this mediated manner on a political or artistic truth procedure. Their action explains how the disruptive elements in neoliberalism and postmodernism, which create circulations in epicyclic form, are even able to arise. Neoliberalism and postmodernism alike were formed in the period of the extinguishing traces of communism and modernism in the 1970s and 1980s. The watershed year of 1989 was the symbolic beginning of a period in which neoliberalism and postmodernism proved that they were the social forces that were rising to dominance. The first period of the interregnum came about, in which the economically and culturally dominant forms had epicycloid shapes. In the beginning of the twenty-first century, they were then transformed, and this is where our present period begins.

Section Two

The Elliptical Period (2000/2008 to the Present)

Introduction

The Path to a Pure Interregnum

We will examine our present time as the second period of the interregnum, in which the traces of the truth procedures have already been extinguished and neoliberal capitalism and postmodernism no longer have their weakened gravitational fields around them. The result of this is that in this period the presence of patterns that used to create the curvature around the circumference of the epicycloid in the first period is weakening and moving toward extinction. The second period can be characterized by the extinction of the peripheral patterns, which changes the character of the core patterns that had been the dominant features of the first period of the interregnum. The second period is already beyond the reach of truth procedures, and because of this "purification," it appears as a period that expresses a purer typology of the interregnum than the one that preceded it. It is only in this period that the character of the patterns and their arrangement crystallizes into what can be considered the typical features of the interregnum. This is when we finally encounter the *interregnum in its pure form*. We can understand the character and arrangement of the patterns that gradually appear before us as representations of the interregnum in its pure form. I'm leaving aside the question of whether we might also detect the presence of patterns of a similar character and arrangement in other interregnum periods in human history. Can we find them in the period of transition between the Middle Ages and the modern period, which in the economic dimension meant a shift from feudalism to early capitalist economic forms? Or will we discover them in the transition from the culture of the late Middle Ages to the Renaissance culture? I recognized their presence in Dante's *Divine Comedy* in the form of infernal formations that have a hybrid nature and make it impossible to determine what is a human being, animal, or plant.[1] However, I have not yet undertaken a sufficient amount of historical research on this subject, so I hesitate to draw more general conclusions. The method of this research may be inspired by Marx, who based his study of the epochs that preceded bourgeois society on the method expressed in his well-known statement that the anatomy of man is the key to the anatomy of the ape. Knowledge of the anatomy of the present period appears as the key to the anatomy of previous periods of transition. However, it is first necessary to examine the anatomy of the present period of transition.

A remarkable phenomenon appears in it, which has not yet been sufficiently captured in either economic or cultural theory. Neoliberalism and postmodernism arrived at a purified state when the trace elements associated with the truth procedures ceased to operate within them. Through this purification, the opposite of what we would expect took place. Instead of their core patterns gaining strength and expanding, they began to fracture internally and collapse, or they mutated. It seems as if liberation from the last traces of communist elements and modernism blocked neoliberalism and postmodernism and then caused their subsequent internal collapse. This phenomenon can be linked to certain symbolic divisions—for neoliberalism, the financial crisis of 2008, and for postmodernism, it was the advent of the new millennium, which marks the beginning of various tracks branching away from postmodernism in the form of a whole series of theoretical and artistic conceptions that proclaim "the end of postmodernism." In the last section, I introduced the epicycloid model, which captured the relationship between core and peripheral patterns. In this section, we will follow the weakening and extinction of the peripheral patterns, which led to a change in the character of the core patterns. If the entire change only consisted in the peripheral patterns ceasing to appear, the epicycloid would transform into a circle. The core patterns would represent the only center of the entire formation, and the deviation from their perimeter caused by the peripheral patterns would cease. In this hypothetical case, we would witness a pure neoliberalism that corresponds to its ideal type. At the same time, we could recognize the pure form of postmodernism, in which the postmodern patterns of diversity, radical plurality, deconstruction, and rhizomatism were delinked from their modernist supplements and shadow categories. The circle as a model that illustrates the pure form of neoliberalism and postmodernism raises the question of whether their pure forms are possible at all in principle. I agree with Jameson, Toth, and Huyssen that neoliberalism and postmodernism cannot exist in pure forms. I have justified this by saying that they arose in the period when the truth procedures were becoming extinct and their "impure" effect is constitutive for them.

In this chapter, we will first observe the transformation of neoliberalism's core patterns in relation to the weakening and extinction of its peripheral patterns. We will focus on the transformation of the neoliberal subject as the dominant pattern, in which the influence of the weakening or extinction of the principle of capitalized citizenship and merit causes it to fracture. Two poles are formed, neither of which is in the core or the peripheral position. Another pattern of neoliberalism that we will examine is the free market. We will also see it splitting into two poles without core and peripheral positions. In the next chapter, we will then look at the formations and phenomena that arise in culture and politics after the end of postmodernism. Here, too, there are poles without a center, which arose as the result of a mutation of the core patterns of postmodernism. As we will see, these poles can be illustrated using an ellipse, which provides a model of shapes that have two constitutive poles and no center. The ellipse depicts the result of implosion and gravitational collapse in economics and culture in the period that extends into the present.

1

Fractured Neoliberalism

The Neoliberal Subject and the End of Merit

In neoliberalism, the principles of capitalized citizenship and merit weakened and became extinct during the 1990s, as we have witnessed in the privatization and tunneling of businesses, and as the ever-widening chasm in income and property between a tiny handful of the extremely wealthy and the rest of society shows. However, the financial crisis in 2008 made the extinction of capitalized citizenship and merit visible. As Wendy Brown writes, the neoliberal discourse on austerity fundamentally differs from Thatcher's and Reagan's neoliberal discourse, in which the promise that wealth was going to trickle down from the wealthiest citizens to all the rest was predominant. As stated above, early neoliberalism promised the population a general increase in wealth. Brown argues that this was a social contract that consisted in the human being, as a neoliberal subject, becoming his or her own enterprise for which they are individually responsible, and the political representation ensures that they will be protected from fatal risks that the subject is not responsible for. In the neoliberal discourse of austerity that emerged during the financial crisis, this promise disappears, and economic goals no longer concern a promise of general wealth increase. Citizens are instead called upon to make a "shared sacrifice" in order to restore the economy to health without being able to demand any future gains as individuals from the sacrifice.[1] Merit, as a correlation between the qualities of human capital and the rewards given by the invisible hand of the market, has disintegrated. The human being as self-investing human capital lives with the knowledge that investment in their competencies, for instance, in the form of education, doesn't necessarily bring any benefit to their "exchange value" or their "use value." In the neoliberal conception of the human being, a fracturing takes place within the very core of the category of human capital. Individual ownership of one's own abilities and work—human capital—is disconnected from the perspective of gain. The citizen is exposed to the requirement of shared sacrifice for a "healthy economy." The individual hand of the market must be complemented by an ethical challenge to self-sacrifice for the sake of the whole, which was not present among the ethical values of early neoliberalism. Brown has observed a fracture in the concept of human capital. Thus, an antinomy has formed within neoliberal discourse, in which individual gain from one's own human capital is in conflict with self-sacrifice without the hope of profit. This antinomy can be generalized as a conflict between the pattern of individual interest and the pattern of general interest. Instead of regulating both of these poles through the invisible market, which transforms individual benefit into general benefit, a gap appears in this neoliberal discourse. The general benefit of a "healthy economy" requires sacrifice of individual interest through austerity measures. In the chapter on early neoliberalism, we saw that the category of individual interest itself is internally fractured because it lacks an autonomously acting bearer who would be the author of decisions made independently of the market. Individual interest has formed in relation to the exchange value of human capital in such a manner that individual interest became that which increases the exchange value of human capital. Exchange value, as an abstract expression for the market relationship of supply and demand, is a social value; therefore, individual interest was formed in relation to the market, which is the basis of social regulation in the neoliberal vision. However, the austerity measures in neoliberalism have in reality only revealed this paradoxical character of individual interest. Healing the economy, which requires austerity measures, shapes individual interest in a similar manner to the way the market used to shape it: it is now in the individual's interest to "share the sacrifice." In this sense, the antinomy of austerity neoliberalism is merely a further development of the antinomy of individual interest that already existed in neoliberalism in its first phase because even then the individual was shaped according to the neoliberal form of governance.

Now let us take a look at specific methods and approaches that are applied in the second phase of neoliberalism, in which the peripheral patterns of capitalized citizenship and merit that still bore traces of communist elements no longer operate. Brown describes three interrelated approaches that distinguish the neoliberal form of governance in the period of the financial crisis after 2008. These are the individualization of responsibility (responsibilization), decentralization of decision-making connected with a transfer of responsibility to a lower level (devolution), and the implementation of "best practices." These are approaches that already appeared in the previous stage of neoliberalism, but now they have intensified and lost their supplements in which the traces of communist elements were still operating.

The Individualization of Responsibility as Capitalist Buddhism

The first approach is to strengthen the individualization of responsibility (responsibilization). This approach is applied when neoliberal policies and economic practices make individuals as "responsible" as possible for their situation and prospects, without regard for their real possibilities, social position, and economic or life contingencies.[2] The individualization of responsibility brings with it a moralization of economic behavior that accompanies the economization of politics.[3] The neoliberal subject is no longer to be understood only as self-investing capital that pursues individual gain because now a moral category of responsibility is supposed to take root within it. The human being as self-investing capital will no longer be guided only by his or her individualism, but they will also take on an ethic of responsibility. It calls on individuals to accept austerities that limit their individual human capital but allegedly contribute to the "recovery" of the economy as a whole. As Wendy Brown says, *Homo economicus* no longer has individual interest at its center, because it no longer has a center.[4] The individualization of responsibility is a neoliberal practice that reacts to the weakening or even the disappearance of a correlation between the work invested in one's own human capital and the gain or returns the human capital should bring. The invisible hand of the market fails because it ceases to ensure this correlation with merit. Neoliberalism used to relate it to the invisible hand of the market as a spontaneous order that provides economic justice without any political power engaging in "social engineering." The failure of the invisible hand of the market was that in the period of the financial crisis that began in 2008, European governments considered it necessary to introduce austerity measures, and they poured massive infusions of money from public treasuries into rehabilitating the banking sector. This political activity went beyond merely creating and maintaining conditions for a market economy that expresses the peripheral etatist principle of neoliberalism discussed above. The state's activity during the financial crisis of 2008 was a manifestation of a sovereign political actor that was supposed to, in an all-too-visible way, heal the invisible hand of the market that, instead of creating spontaneous order, made a chasm that the whole economy might fall into if it remained "spontaneous."

This was not an activity that creates conditions for the market to operate, which would be in line with the principles of neoliberalism; rather, it was compensating losses in the banking sector that had been caused by the free market while at the same time imposing restrictions that affected the other sectors of the economy. However, if this hadn't been done, the collapse of the whole economy was to be expected. The failure of the invisible hand of the market made it necessary to restore the role of the state as a political sovereign in the interest of preserving at least a few of the core principles of neoliberalism. But these core principles then began to fracture.

The neoliberal subject should accept the ethic of individual responsibility because the faith in merit as a correlation between investment in one's own human capital and the returns from these investments was no longer there. The ethic of responsibility is a reaction to the loss of faith in merit, which had constituted a peripheral pattern to neoliberalism. The neoliberal ethic of responsibility reacts to the failure of the invisible hand of the market and performs an operation in which the correlation of merit between labor and gain is canceled, because the financial crisis showed that the market does not create a spontaneous *order* that ensures the correlation with merit, and therefore also provides neoliberal economic justice. However, there is no other instance that would create this order. We can see the demystification of the market that Marx called for taking place right within neoliberalism. The result is an individualization of responsibility that leads to the neoliberal subject no longer being able to rely on the invisible hand of the market. The correlation with merit was an ethical principle that acted outside the will of individuals. However, the free market ethically foundered because the correlation with merit, and thus also spontaneous economic justice, collapsed. The ethic is thus transferred from the market to the individual. The neoliberal subject is expected to take on the ethic of responsibility and sacrifice because the market has proven to be unethical.

The ethic of individualized responsibility requires the neoliberal subject to refrain from blaming any external instance, whether the market, the state, or a corporation, for the fact that they cannot count on a correlation between their labor and their gains. The ethical imperative is: "Don't blame anyone else if merit no longer applies." If the neoliberal subject, as self-investing human capital, founders despite the maximal investment of capacities and abilities, this result must be taken as an expression of an imponderable way of the world that is not controlled by the human, all-too-human criterion of merit and justice. From the perspective of the ethic of individualized responsibility, it appears as a promise connected with "anthropocentrism" and "the human perspective."

Contemporary neoliberalism leads us to adopt a "posthuman" perspective, which allegedly advances the too-limited human perspective. The rejection of anthropocentrism is an answer to the failure of the market, which contained the "anthropocentric" ethics of merit and justice. One of the other forms, and the most widespread one, is "Western Buddhism," which offers as its main pearl of wisdom that the free and emotional center of the human being remains empty and that individual interest appears to us as clinging to something non-essential. This Buddhism is the spiritual ideology of disintegrating neoliberalism.

The Disintegration of Neoliberalism and Self-sacrifice

Wendy Brown emphasizes that the ethic of individualized responsibility has another dimension: willingness for self-sacrifice. The concept of sacrifice is seen as complementary to the neoliberal economic logic that is inconsistent and requires an ethical position that allows it to renew a "healthy" economy and avert currency collapse, debt insolvency, and state bankruptcy. This sacrifice is not made for the nation or the demos, but "for a spectacularly arranged state and economy, upon which everything living depends, but which at the same time causes destruction and hardship."[5] The call to self-sacrifice is de facto a call to suppress the fundamental principle of neoliberalism, which is the maximization of personal benefit, which is to say the pursuit of personal interest.[6] The neoliberal subject has been inconsistent since the beginning, as we have seen in the chapter on neoliberalism in the first period of the interregnum. It was not based in use value that consists in the autonomous experience of the usefulness of things, but in an exchange relationship that defines the value of the subject as human capital. The neoliberal subject did not have an autonomous "center" inside itself from which unique longings and desires would be born. The exchange relationship as a basis for self-investing capital already expresses the principle of sacrifice, in which self-limitation or self-repression correlates with the expected profit. Capitalist exchange continues the ancient principle of sacrifice, in which the exchange relationship was already operating, as Adorno and Horkheimer write in *Dialectic of Enlightenment*.[7] The difference lies in the contemporary sacrifice lacking this character of exchange, because individuals should sacrifice themselves in order to bring the economy back to health and accept austerities without expecting any instance in which they will be rewarded for their sacrifice. In contemporary neoliberalism, as a result of the extinction of the principle of merit, the exchange relationship is lost as a regulator of self-investing capital. Exchange as the basis of the neoliberal subject collapses. Instead of a commodity exchange that operates on the basis of the principle of equivalence, as Marx described in his theory of value, a call is issued to human capital to sacrifice itself (along with all the others) without compensation for its investment. This is exchange without equivalence, in which instead of the expected use, a kind of nonauthoritarian ideological call for common self-sacrifice for the sake of bringing the society's economy back to health. The human being as self-investing capital fractures internally into a being with individualized responsibility who should invest in its competencies, and a being that sacrifices its capital to the interest of the whole. The neoliberal subject has split. On the one hand, the subject should apply herself without the support of collective organizations and common institutions, and on the other, she should be responsible for the whole economy and accept self-limitation, precarious life conditions, and every other call for self-sacrifice. In this call to sacrifice, Brown sees the beginning of a convergence of neoliberalism with fascism, where the individual also had to sacrifice himself for the higher good of the collective, without expectation that his self-sacrifice would bring any personal benefit. This author does not claim that neoliberalism is fascism, or that we are living in a fascist period, because neoliberalism is still functioning without an authoritative state and a dictatorial political regime.[8] However, the neoliberal call for self-sacrifice is one of the main moments in the conservative turn, which has the character of a movement toward collectively shared values, such as national identity. Neoliberalism in a state of disintegration encourages discourse on "ethical values" connected with the conservative turn. And because it has given impetus to a conservative turn, certain conservative populists (such as Jair Bolsonaro in Brazil and Thierry Baudet in the Netherlands) openly call it an ally in the return to conservative values. By contrast, other conservative populists (such as Orbán and the representatives of the Polish Law and Justice party) build their politics on social motifs and make social transfers to particular groups in the population. These forms of politics are reacting to the asocial consequences of the breakdown of neoliberalism, while the politics of Bolsonaro and Baudet are faithful to neoliberalism as an impetus toward a conservative turn.

Self-sacrifice in neoliberalism means accepting austerity measures, precarious work, or unemployment without expressions of disapproval. By contrast with fascism, the willingness for self-sacrifice is not induced by exhibitions of a commonly joined will, which is what the fascist and Nazi mass parades that embodied the national community were. Brown is partially right when she writes that *Homo economicus* no longer has individual interest at its center, because it has lost its center.[9] This finding can be connected with the specific character of self-sacrifice in neoliberalism. If the neoliberal subject lacks a relationship to its own individual interest, self-sacrifice isn't commanded, or, strictly speaking, isn't the result of an ideological appeal. Brown inclines toward the idea that in neoliberalism an ideological appeal is operating that inspires a willingness to self-sacrifice, but—in keeping with Althusser's theory of ideology—this appeal assumes a symbolic authority of the institutions that issue it. Demonstrably, however, neoliberalism has dismantled this symbolic authority or Lacanian "symbolic order." Therefore, it cannot rely on an authoritative call for self-sacrifice.[10] Neoliberalism awakens the will to self-sacrifice by bringing in an ethical element that is foreign to neoliberal doctrine: the appeal to the common interest and the whole economy. There is a contradictory operation taking place, in which the foreign element of the common interest and the whole economy arouses a will to self-sacrifice, which is supposed to save neoliberalism.

"Best Practices" as a Neoliberal Ethic of Unification

The concept of general interest and of the whole economy is fundamental for understanding the relationship between unity and plurality, which is formed as a special effect of neoliberal individualizing practices. Brown expresses this relationship as *omnes et singulatim*, or "all and each one," which represents both the mass and isolation.[11] She explains this phenomenon as a result of the individualization of responsibility and the decentralization of decision-making, which is connected with a transfer of responsibility to a lower level (devolution) and with the implementation of "best practices."

A practice that creates a principle of neoliberal unification is one that can be considered a "best practice." The term "best practices" refers to approaches, processes, and methods of management that were successful in certain types of organizations from the perspective of neoliberal rationality, and therefore they are transferred into other types of organizations. They form templates that are beginning to be used universally in all kinds of organizations, not only corporations focused on profit but also in nonprofit organizations and universities. "Best practices" seem like a non-normative guide for how to organize an organization's management and administration processes seemingly in the best possible way. These templates are created by experts in collaboration with people who have practical experience, and they give the impression of being the best possible result of an alliance of theory and practice that represents expert knowledge as well as practical experience. "Best practices" become a generally applied template that applies many neoliberal methods. They assert soft power, seem to be apolitical, create consensus, inspire teamwork, introduce market metrics, and reject regulation by command. "Best practices" are a tool to introduce market thinking into the public sphere and into activities that previously had not been subject to market criteria.[12]

In the late 1980s, Fredric Jameson wrote about late capitalism, in which exchange expanded into areas that previously had partial autonomy; that is, it entered art, the unconscious, and nature.[13] However, there were still institutions and activities that had maintained a partially autonomous form of rationality, such as the university and volunteer organizations. However, "best practices" change them by introducing a depoliticized ethic of consensus, which is connected with postmodern culture. The dissolution of boundaries between the political and economic systems and the partially autonomous areas weakened the capability of keeping a critical distance and created a depoliticized ethics of consensus. The depoliticized ethics of consensus then created conditions in which market rationality appears to be ubiquitous and natural because it represents a generally shared structure of thinking, experiencing, and acting. The ethic of consensus bases its appeals on its apolitical, nonhierarchical, and nondogmatic nature, which gives the impression that "best practices" is not only a tool of capitalist management but expresses emancipatory and humanist values. "Best practices" thus builds upon previous managerial and regulatory approaches that reshaped the anti-hierarchical and anti-authoritarian imperatives from the 1968 protest movements for their purpose, as discussed in the chapter on neoliberalism with communist elements.[14]

"Best practices" thus acts as a template, thanks to which its consensual, anti-hierarchical, and nonideological ethic is not experienced as part of the capitalist form of domination. However, there is a split within it. It is a template that arises as an allegedly depoliticized approach that is free of dogma, prejudice, and rigid commands, but on the other hand, it is applied in a manner that fails to take the dimension of a particular field of activity's content into account. For example, this takes place when practices developed in the aeronautics or computer industry are transferred to educational or healthcare institutions. "Best practices" eliminate everything that guided a particular institution in its history, such as traditional approaches or values, as the first order of business.[15] This enforced caesura suggests that the "best practices" have the character of suppressing whatever doesn't correspond to the proven template of "best practices." "Best practices" can therefore be understood as an alienated general rule. At the same time, however, this alienation is legitimized by its allegedly anti-authoritarian, consensual, and nonideological nature. There is a fracture here, which we have already seen in the neoliberal subject in the chapter on the first period of neoliberalism. The human being voluntarily assumes the form of the neoliberal subject, but this voluntary acceptance is the result of the type of pressure that I have termed situational determination. You don't have to accept this form, but if you don't, you will face certain consequences. A certain gap thus remains between the human being and the neoliberal subject, which can be activated under certain circumstances. We find a similar situational determination with "best practices." A particular organization isn't bound to accept it, but if it doesn't, its rating will be lowered, which reduces its competitiveness and weakens its position in the market. The continual comparison of nonprofit public institutions, such as universities, is done on the basis of benchmarks that are not derived from the specific content and the ideal of education, humanism, and critical thinking, because these are quantitative indicators where it is unclear what, exactly, is being measured, as Konrad Liessmann writes.[16] Educational and healthcare institutions are examples of organizations whose activity doesn't create products in the form of goods whose value is quantitative; rather, they are educational processes and services that will always escape the schematism of classifying goods. However, the "best practices" approach subjects these institutions to the same processes as industrial enterprises that produce commodities.

The comparative measuring of universities or healthcare institutions on the basis of this kind of neoliberal approach assumes that these organizations are focusing on the projection of some kind of quantitatively measurable units (commodities). However, owing to the nature of their activities, these institutions cannot be entirely transformed into industrial enterprises that manufacture goods. There is always a discrepancy between the result of their activity and the quantification methods applied by the neoliberal style of evaluation. Comparative measurement on the basis of quantifying benchmarks is modeled according to the principle of exchange, but this is an odd case of measurement that disrupts the idea of an exchange relation as a relationship between quantifiable units. Neoliberal measurement in these non-market areas is an example of what has always eluded quantification to a certain extent, and therefore the exchange relations are always dislocated here. "Best practices," a methodology that transfers approaches and benchmarks from one field to all the others, creates a discrepancy between a generally applicable template and the content, goals, and principles of activity in fields that are exposed to this template and forced to adapt to it. The promotion of this template is reminiscent of a kind of pseudo-revolutionary act of separation from the previous era, in which the discontinuity between the new and the old world is established. In this area, "best practices" and benchmarking evoke the impression of a certain revolutionary dynamism that can be understood as an example of the neoliberal transformation of the Maoist spirit of 1968, whose revolutionary elan has been depoliticized and translated into principles of management for companies and public institutions.

Unifying Practices as a Fracturing of Neoliberalism

"Best practices" are management templates that apply certain practical approaches to help bring about a neoliberal form of unification. Examining these templates provides a guide for understanding the assemblage nature of this unification, where we find elements that are foreign to one another. I thus supplement Wendy Brown's analysis, which focuses on the contradictory effects of the crisis of neoliberal rationality, but did not examine the distortion of the character of the unification that forms the "whole" in neoliberal discourse. We can conceive of the self-sacrifice for the sake of the "whole of the healthy economy" that Brown writes about using the example of "best practices" as a unifying template for management. The outlines of the whole arise as a result of the demise of the "invisible hand of the market" as a harmonizing principle that was a manifestation of neoliberal utopianism, as I wrote in the previous chapter. We can now track how a split in the core neoliberal concept of the market takes place after the demise of the harmonizing function of the "invisible hand of the market." Instead of the market as an aggregate of individual actors and their interests, expressed through the relationship between supply and demand, two poles emerge that are in an antinomical relationship but act upon one another. The market still remains an aggregate of individual actors and their interests, but at the same time, after the demise of the harmonizing "invisible hand," a change from a mere aggregate to a certain whole that is expressed through the concept of the "whole healthy economy" takes place. This whole can be characterized on the basis of approaches and aspects that we have encountered with Brown and other authors.

"Best practices" represents a symptomatic practice of unification that causes a suppression of the past in a pseudo-revolutionary dynamic spirit. This practice introduces a template that is a form of separation from the content or character of a product and activity and evokes a requirement for a consensus that is based on an ethic of being "the best." A concept of a whole arises that is the result of stitching together separate spheres of activity and life. It is a sewing that is done with the help of the "best practices" template as a practical form of unification, in which unity is not created as an organic unification of various elements, but it is a heterogeneous unity in which, paradoxically, the individual areas of activity move apart from one another and become more isolated the more they are unified on the basis of neoliberal management templates. The contents, values, and forms of activities in individual areas (universities, healthcare institutions, human rights organizations) cannot be entirely suppressed, because this would result in a loss of their purpose for existence. However, the neoliberal template imprinted on them with benchmarks for their evaluation and competitiveness compares things that don't correspond to the content and form of their activity, as Liessman illustrates. Indicators that are poorly matched with the character of these areas are compared. The neoliberal template thus forms a network of relationships that are practiced in a distorted manner because they don't arise on the basis of benchmarks or formal-content sides that would correspond to the character of the areas that are entering into mutual relationship. The neoliberal template is the bearer of a unification that is disproportionate to the areas that are thus linked, even though it is represented as the "best practice." It is even possible to consider that the more this template is applied in further areas, the more the specific contents, values, and principles of these areas are suppressed. The neoliberal template is the bearer of a unification that is only possible under the fulfillment of the condition that a suppression of specific contents and principles in the given area has taken place. Thus, a gap appears between the general (neoliberal template) and the individual.

The Consensual Ethic of Contemporary Neoliberalism

Another feature of the neoliberal creation of the whole is its ethic of a pseudo-revolutionary dimension connected with anti-hierarchical, anti-authoritarian, and anti-elite values. This dimension is related to the notion that the whole of the "healthy economy" emerges non-politically and without ideological prejudices. Expert knowledge, tested and adjusted in company practice, soft methods of management that avoid direct commands, ethical codices, and other similar methods bring the idea of good, or even the greatest possible good, the *best* practices into neoliberal rationality. If we realize that this belief in the invisible hand of the market also contained an ethical element (the correlation between diligence and reward), the neoliberal ethics of goodness, connected with the pseudo-revolutionary anti-hierarchicalism, can be understood as a surrogate of this lost faith. Instead of providence and similar metaphysical categories that served in the history of capital as an ethical impulse to doing business or to identifying with capitalist subjectivity, here we encounter a non-metaphysical ethical incentive to self-sacrifice. Some authors have pointed out that the invisible hand of the market is a metaphysical concept. For example, on the basis of a conceptual genealogy, Giorgio Agamben shows that the neoliberal "spontaneous order" has a teleological origin and character. This concept is based on the idea of a "natural order" created by God. The invisible hand of the market replaces God and forms a "spontaneous order."[17] It would certainly be worth a closer investigation into whether this metaphysics of the invisible hand of the market that revived neoliberalism isn't a reaction to Stalinist metaphysics. History as a dialectical order which is the guarantor of an evolution toward communism. However, the neoliberal whole economy no longer conceals the metaphysics of the invisible hand of the market. Its highest possible good is construed as an expression of the practices which have "best proven themselves." However, this practice erases the promise of a correlation with merit, which was connected to the invisible hand of the market. The neoliberal whole of the "healthy economy" doesn't offer the semblance of promises that human self-investing capital will be rewarded with profit.

Here we see how "best practices" complement the "individualization of responsibility." The neoliberal subject has internally fracted into self-investing capital that pursues the individual perspective of acting, and an ethical subject that practices self-sacrifice for the sake of the whole "healthy economy." The ethical appeal to the neoliberal subject arises out of the demise of the harmonizing role of the invisible hand of the market. Instead of this harmonizing instance, the notion of the whole "healthy economy" appears, which requires self-sacrifice. This demand then causes fracturing to take place within the neoliberal subject into the individual criterion of success and the perspective of the economic whole. This is a consequence of the fracturing of characteristics within the market itself, which continues to express the individual actions of economic actors, but at the same time is conceived and shaped as a "whole."

The split in the terms "market" and "neoliberal subject," which are the core patterns of neoliberalism, takes yet another form. The neoliberal subject, as an individual actor, continues to pursue the "selfish" impulses of the previous phase of neoliberalism, but as a self-sacrificing actor, it accepts the principle of consensus and shapes its behavior in conformity with consensus thinking, which is justified by antihierarchicalism and anti-authoritarianism. Consensus thinking means that the neoliberal subject prioritizes decision-making by groups above decision-making undertaken on the basis of individual interest. Consensus creates pressure on individual aspirations to excel in creativity and thus gain a more advantageous position than others, according to the neoliberal ethic of the previous stage. Consensus thinking is becoming the new ethic of neoliberalism. Consensus and group thinking generally are manifestations of the weakening of the individualist side of the neoliberal subject, which Brown describes as a disappearance of the center—which used to be the site where individual preferences were formed—in the neoliberal subject. As this author emphasizes, no collective sensibility arises; instead, it is only a mechanism of cooperation among individuals who remain isolated from one another. Neoliberal consensus thinking does not disturb the individualistic character of the neoliberal subject, but it evokes the idea of an ethical obligation of conformity with the whole. A paradoxical element of the neoliberal consensus is that conformism is legitimized on the basis of transmuted anti-hierarchical and anti-authoritarian imperatives that appeared in the radical emancipatory movements of 1968. The ethic of consensus even, from a certain point of view, appears as a proto-totalitarian manner of decision-making, in which dissenting perspectives are a priori considered unethical. Whoever refuses to participate in a given procedure of creating consent is suspected of hidden elitist or authoritarian tendencies. Here, we are encountering a proto-totalitarian form of thinking, in which the originality, imagination, and creativity of the individual are winnowed by the group perspective and must be adapted depending on whether the group arrives at an agreement, which is a more ethically valuable principle than the most admirable contributions of an individual.

Another instrument of neoliberal rationality in the state of fracturing is "consensual voting," in which a decision can only be adopted if all the participants agree with it. During the voting, a single "nay" suffices for the group to reject the proposal without there being any need to justify the negative vote. It isn't necessary to refine arguments in a back-and-forth polemic, because the mere utterance of disagreement with a proposal suffices. The results are thus based on the form of the voting as such, and not on arguments that have won majority support. Consensual voting expresses the residual role of the individual in neoliberal rationality. The individual can overturn a consensual decision made by the majority by expressing disagreement. The conclusion is that no consensus has been reached and the decision is not accepted. However, this is only a residual role for the individual, because the individual only retains this role *negatively*. He confirms his role in the act of a rejection that he needn't justify. Thus, there appears a residual individuality that is not based on individual abilities, ideas, or the strength of argument, but only in the expression of disagreement. In this way, consensual thinking helps form a type of individual that corresponds to neoliberalism in the stage of fracturing. The fractured neoliberal subject lacks a center and has been emptied of content. It can confirm its existence through negative acts of disagreement. Neoliberal consensus thinking is fractured: on the one hand, the individual can confirm their individuality during a vote if they express a different standpoint than the others; on the other, those who are participating in the voting lose their will to argue, because argumentation and justification of a dissenting position appear like ethically problematic expressions of elitism. Consensus thinking thus leads to decisions that are not the result of rational discussion where there is a struggle between arguments. This match or struggle is usually led from certain *different* perspectives, which usually remain different even when the majority decides. However, consensus voting assumes a final agreement even of these sides. Otherwise, it only forces the participants to suppress their positions or deny them in the interest of reaching consensus. Therefore, consensus decision-making appears to be a type of decision-making involving a formal consensus-building process, which may not be rational at all in the sense of how justifiable the proposal under consideration may be. From this perspective, neoliberal consensus thinking can be understood as a group-legitimized suppression of the contents of thought that has to do with the matter itself. Consensus thinking is in this way similar to "best practices," which introduce an approach in which the specific contents of a given sphere of activity are procedurally suppressed. Consensus thinking and "best practices" create a certain form of generality that is distinguished by a disrupted or alienated relationship to the uniqueness of objects and activities that they regulate or evaluate.

The Split of the Market and the Neoliberal Subject into Two Poles

The splits in the market model and in the neoliberal subject, which are the core patterns of neoliberalism, offer us the possibility of more clearly sketching the contours of this *omnes et singulatim* that Brown writes about. The word *omnes* symbolically expresses the neoliberal whole and the unifying practices whose characteristics have already been introduced. At the discursive level, this whole appears as the whole of the "healthy economy," by which is meant an economy that fulfills the neoliberal requirement of fiscal discipline and a balanced state budget. However, it is not appropriate to limit the neoliberal conception of the whole economy to purely economic criteria. Let's summarize our findings on this matter: we have examined the allegedly apolitical "ethical" character of the whole economy. Neoliberalism represents this economic whole as an apolitical formation in which ideology and doctrines have lost their former significance. It acquires its ethical character by shaping itself through "best practices" and consensus thought, in which appear transmuted elements of antihierarchicalism and anti-authoritarianism that arose in the movement in 1968. Its seemingly apolitical and de-ideologized character acquires an ethical dimension thanks to approaches such as soft management, communication, and the implementation of proven practices under expert guidance. In neoliberalism, other forms of unifying concepts with a certain ethical charge appear at the discursive level, such as the "national interest," which the icon of Czech neoliberal politics, Václav Klaus, has begun to speak about. In neoliberalism, a tendency appears to create unifying concepts that distort and fracture the original understanding of the market as a spontaneously arising harmonization of individual interests, activities, and needs expressed through supply and demand. Thatcher expressed this spirit of neoliberalism through her famous statement "there is no such thing as society," which we can also interpret as the thesis "the whole doesn't exist." The creation of unifying concepts and the idea of the economic whole appears as a denial of Thatcher's statement by neoliberalism itself. Unifying concepts such as the "national interest" and the idea of the economic whole are the result of processes that led to a disintegration of belief in the harmonizing role of the invisible hand of the market that guaranteed merit and a correlation between self-investment and rewards in the form of profit. The principle of merit expresses the egalitarian element of neoliberalism which came to prevail in it as a reaction to the traces of the communist idea still present in society, as was discussed in the previous chapter. We can illustrate the whole process through the fact that in the present period of interregnum merit, which in the previous epicyclical period had represented a peripheral model, has become extinct as an egalitarian element of neoliberalism. However, its extinction has influenced the core pattern of the free market in its harmonizing function. As a result of the extinction of merit as an expression of the harmonizing function, the free market pattern splits into two poles. The first pole expresses the character of the market as an aggregate of individual interests and activities, while the second pole represents unification and the whole, in which the above-mentioned "non-merit" ethic of good appears.

The term *singulatim* refers to the second core pattern: the neoliberal subject. On the basis of previous investigations, I have come to the conclusion that the extinction of the neoliberal peripheral patterns of merit and capitalized citizenship also affects the neoliberal subject: it is also split into two poles. One pole expresses the continuation of neoliberal individualism focused on profit. The other one is formed through unifying practices and the creation of the idea of the economic whole. Because of this pole, the neoliberal subject makes sacrifices and denies the imperative of individual profit. As stated before, neoliberal self-sacrifice happens because of the failure of the invisible hand of the market as a guarantee of correlation through merit. The failure of the market manifests as a weakening and then extinguishing of the principle of merit, which also changes the character of the neoliberal subject, which is now exposed to the requirement of the individualization of responsibility. In our examination of the transformation of the neoliberal subject, we have discovered that the individualization of responsibility means self-sacrifice. After the breakdown of the principle of merit, the neoliberal subject creates a distance between itself and their individual interest because they are aware that their individual interest can still be annulled, despite all their investments into their own capital. The neoliberal subject individualizes responsibility for their own failure and doesn't blame the market or any other instance. If they were harboring a belief that the invisible hand of the market is guaranteed by merit, they couldn't move into the position of self-sacrificing for the whole of the "healthy economy." The subject would understand this whole as being unjust and failing to fulfill neoliberalism's promises. Therefore, the individualism of responsibility is a condition so that the neoliberal subject will sacrifice itself for the health of the economic whole. As it turned out, neoliberal self-sacrifice corresponds to the exchange relationship ceasing to be the regulator of self-investing capital. Individual interest and exchange no longer make up the core of the neoliberal subject because this subject consensually sacrifices itself along with the others without compensation for their investment. The center of the neoliberal subject remains empty in a fundamental sense. It doesn't contain either capital and its exchange or self-sacrifice. After the breakdown of the correlation with merit as a surrogate for communist elements, the neoliberal subject splits into the pole of self-investing capital and the pole of self-sacrifice for the sake of the economic whole. Neither one nor the other of these poles forms the center of the neoliberal subject.

To summarize: the expression *omnes et singulatim* as a characteristic of contemporary neoliberalism is oddly fractured. *Omnes* as a symbol of neoliberal society has a large fracture within it, which divides it into two poles. One of these is the free market as an aggregate of individual interests, and the other is composed of unifying practices and the economic whole. *Singulatim*, which expresses the neoliberal subject, also splits into two poles in the same way. The first is the individual interest of human capital, and the second is self-sacrifice for the economic whole. The *Omnes et singulatim* are in this manner internally fractured and lacking centers. As we will see below, these poles are in positions that correspond to the position of the foci in the ellipse.

The Infernal Character of Contemporary Neoliberalism

In this chapter, we have examined the transformation of the core patterns of the market and the neoliberal subject in a period that began with the financial crisis of 2008. The correlation function of merit and other peripheral patterns of neoliberalism weakens and becomes extinct because the traces of the communist idea whose sequence was symbolically closed in 1989, have. We have observed the hitherto insufficiently described phenomenon of the fracturing of the core patterns of neoliberalism, which have occurred as a consequence of the loss of its peripheral patterns. The "free market" has split into a pole that is a continuation of the original neoliberal conception of the market as an aggregate of individual interests that enter into exchange relations, and a pole of the economic whole, which demands self-sacrifice from individual actors. The neoliberal subject is divided into self-investing capital that pursues individual profit and the self-sacrificing individual that pursues the common good. As a result of the fracturing, the economy has two poles and no center, because the core patterns of neoliberalism have fractured and there is no pattern that now makes up its core. The free market can only exist over the long term if there is a healthy economic whole, and vice versa: a healthy economic whole can only exist if there is a free market. The case is similar with the neoliberal subject. The individual interest of the neoliberal subject is conditional upon it performing self-sacrifice in the interest of helping the economic whole to heal. However, self-sacrifice is an action done for the benefit of the economic whole, which relies upon the individual interest of economic actors. A healthy economic whole is conditioned by the free market as an aggregate of individual interests. The healthy economic whole expresses the general interest, which is a category that was alien to early neoliberalism. The demand for self-sacrifice is likewise alien in neoliberalism. These categories cannot be derived from the original core patterns of the "free market" and the "neoliberal subject." What, then, is indicated by the fact that, after the extinction of the peripheral patterns of merit and the equal opportunity of capitalized citizenship has taken place, the core formulas split and have linked up with patterns alien to them? The peripheral patterns also originated outside of neoliberalism, because they arose as reactions to the presence of communist traces in the society of the 1970s and 1980s. These patterns disappeared, but other alien patterns had to appear in order for the free market and the neoliberal subject to continue to exist, albeit in a changed form. This requirement for alien patterns suggests that neoliberalism cannot manage without prostheses as a necessary condition of its existence. The prosthetic or "impure" character of neoliberalism indicates the more general character of the period of the interregnum.

The continued existence of neoliberalism today is conditioned by the spread of certain ethical values. This doesn't only refer to the call to self-sacrifice but an overall ethical turn that is manifested in political rhetoric. In his *Second Manifesto for Philosophy*, Badiou writes about the increase in moralizing preaching about good and evil, for instance, in connection with the "war against terrorism." According to Badiou, a mixture of conservative morality and political conformism is emerging after a period in which everything seemed to be relative.[18] However, I do not see this ethical turn only as a change in the political world but mainly as a manifestation of the crisis of neoliberalism, which has created the need to use ethical values to support it. The spread of ethical values and moralizing sermons is a symptom of the second period of the interregnum, in which the traces of the communist idea whose sequence closed in 1989 were extinguished. However, these ethical values are not strong enough to create dominant or core patterns. The present economy lacks core values, and its center remains empty. This is why there are frequent switches from the repertoire of the original neoliberal patterns (the market, efficiency, competition, capital) to a repertoire of ethical patterns and patterns that express the common good (self-sacrifice, the good of the whole, the national interest, or the nation state), and vice versa. There is a constant circulation between the first and second repertoires of patterns.

This is reminiscent of the circulation that was described in the cultural sphere by Timotheus Vermeulen and Robin van den Akker in their model of two poles that express the "metamodernism" discussed at the conclusion of the section devoted to the first period of the interregnum. We can illustrate the relationship between the poles using the model of the ellipse, which will be presented in the last part of this section. The model of the ellipse expresses the dependence of each concept that arises in the present economy on both poles. Economic visions that come close to the original neoliberal patterns always depend on the second pole, which is the common interest and the ethics of the "good." The same is true of the opposite circulation, which is operated by conservative populism. This movement approaches the pole of the common good and the ethics of "good" in its rhetoric when it speaks of collective identities, the nation, or the people. However, at the same time, it is dependent on neoliberalism's original patterns, and its dependence always becomes evident; for example, by promoting competitiveness as a national interest.

This elliptical circulation of contemporary neoliberalism means that each promise of improving the personal or social situation issued by neoliberal, or later conservative populist politicians is always broken because the reality of the market returns: competitiveness and private capital that require individuals' self-sacrifice. On the one hand, there are promises of the healing of society or the nation, but on the other, deep insecurity, permanent stress, and self-exploitation prevail, accompanied by frustration that individual efforts don't bring about an improvement in one's life situation. Contemporary neoliberalism creates an ellipse in which the proximity and distance of hope alternate, just like the proximity and distance of despair. Freud's concept of the death instinct, which is manifested in the compulsive repetition of a cycle of coming closer and then distancing oneself from the object of desire, is the figure of thought that expresses these circulations.[19] We can understand this concept of Freud's as a metaphorical expression of a circulation between promises and their frustration when they are reneged on, a circulation between individual interest and the common interest, or a circulation between a plurality of economic actors and the unity of the economic whole. No principle or pattern exists here in such a way that a person might identify with it as a fundamental guiding principle. Getting closer to the "national interest" or another value is always associated with a delay and then a new approach. Through these circulations, contemporary neoliberalism arouses an urge to break down every established principle, value, or pattern, and along with it, there is a desire for extinction, which are qualities that belong to Freud's concept of the death instinct. We can therefore conclude that the elliptical circulation of neoliberalism creates a death instinct whose actions it is unable to sufficiently suppress or overcome. The promises and hopes of fragmented neoliberalism take place in a regime of the death instinct because they are continually drawing closer and then again draw away. Above the entrance to the world of fractured neoliberalism could be the same inscription that hangs over the gate to Hell in Dante's *Divine Comedy*: "Abandon hope, all ye who enter here."

2

Contemporary Culture and Politics as Infinite Circulation

Metamodernism, Remodernism, Altermodernism . . . a Multiplicity of Names for Contemporary Culture

In the section on economics in the current stage of the interregnum, we could notice a certain terminological difficulty. I didn't write about neoliberalism without attributes, but about neoliberalism in a state of fracturing. Other authors who discuss the present form of neoliberalism are also hesitant to use the word "neoliberalism," some choosing neologisms such as ultra-neoliberalism or hyper-neoliberalism. Wendy Brown shows significant differences between Thatcher-Reagan neoliberalism and the present form, but she did not come up with a specific term for it. Neoliberalism has ceased to be a term that can be applied without certain terminological corrections or supplementary commentary, because in the contemporary economy, there are elements of operation that prevent us from using the word without hesitation. Today, there is no comprehensive economic theory that captures in a complex and internally coherent manner all of these various elements and would also provide an apt label for the contemporary economy. We will not find a new economic theory comparable with the neoclassical theory of the Austrian school or Keynes's theory that would also provide a comprehensive theoretical framework for economic policy.[1]

There is a similar situation in cultural theory. The concept of postmodernism today appears to be insufficient or obsolete, but we don't have a more apt term that is close at hand and that we can agree upon that would describe the character of the culture of the past few decades. Although the accuracy of the concept of postmodernism has always been questioned, the term was widely used in the 1980s and 1990s, and even those who criticized the phenomena expressed within this trend use it, such as David Harvey, Terry Eagleton, and Alex

Callinicos. What term should be chosen to describe contemporary culture and how should it be characterized? As Brian McHale aptly wrote in the annotation of the book *Metamodernism: Historicity, Affect, and Depth After Postmodernism*, which represents a representative anthology of texts about art and culture at the beginning of the twentieth century: "If you're looking for a polished, dazzling new aesthetic of this post-post or meta, you won't find it here—however, you won't find it anywhere, because it doesn't exist."[2]

What he termed postmodernism was the culturally dominant form of the 1980s and 1990s, which was illustrated using the epicycloid, in which there are core patterns (radical plurality, singularity, deconstruction, dissemination, the rhizome, irony, etc.) and peripheral patterns made up of the residual or weakened elements of modernism (subversive and anti-system intentions, absolute justice, emancipatory paralogy, euphoria). At least since the beginning of the new millennium, we have been witnessing attempts at conceptually grasping the cultural tendencies that were already emerging in the 1990s, and which cannot be understood as part of postmodern culture, such as the new realism in the fine arts and literature. As the editors of the book *Supplanting the Postmodern* write, today the feeling predominates that postmodernism has ended, but in its place, there appear only experimental definitions of the contemporary situation in art and culture.[3] Trends, aesthetic concepts, and theoretical reflections appear, which emphasize different phenomena and offer mutually incompatible definitions of what's happening in the world of art and culture. Alan Kirby, for example, writes about the significance of digital technology, whereas Vermeulen and van den Akker draw attention to the emergence of a new romanticism. At the same time, points of contact appear in these conceptions and trends which correspond to shared experiences or structures of experience that are being formed and which can gradually create a unifying term for the present culture. Most of the names proposed contain the word modernism: metamodernism, remodernism, altermodernism, automodernism, digimodernism, hypermodernism, transmodernism, pseudomodernism, and we would probably find even more names that would be similar to them. These attempts at naming the current cultural situation correspond to the emergence or strengthening of tendencies and cultural patterns that resemble modernism, but without conceiving of themselves as a simple return to it. The authors of these concepts usually point out that twentieth-century modernism is not returning, because we live in different cultural and political conditions than the ones in which modernism arose. Its newly formed patterns appear in diverse and sometimes inconsistent modulations. Remodernism deals with the new form of artistic autonomy and spiritual intentions of early modernists such as Kandinsky and Eliot, whereas in his conception of pseudomodernism, Kirby speaks critically about the pseudoautonomy created by digital technologies and social media. However, these concepts and trends agree that postmodernism in the form defined by Jameson, Lyotard, and other theorists has become a thing of the past. The end of postmodernism has also been proclaimed by some of the authors who wrote crucial works on the phenomenon of postmodernism itself. Linda Hutcheon, the author of the important book *The Politics of Postmodernism*, writes in the epilogue to its 2002 edition that although postmodernism has been institutionalized its historical moment has passed. We are in a world in which as a result of digitalization and globalization the character of textuality and the overall political context have changed. Ihab Hassan, who has written a number of influential books on literary postmodernism, claims today that it is necessary to renew the qualities of belief and empathy in literature and to abandon the nihilist postmodern notion that no such thing as truth exists. He adds that due to the nihilistic ends of postmodernism, we should renew the relationship to reality.

Simon Critchley noted the symptomatic change in the university environment: "I remember that the graduate students at Essex had begun to organize a radical politics reading group in 1999, which I always attended, and there was a palpable shift in tone and toleration. There was an impatience with deconstruction, which seemed politically irrelevant and textualist, a frustration with the platitudes of post-Structuralist anti-essentialism and what appeared to be its cheerleading for democracy, and the desire for a return to Marx. The stage shifted and a new cast of characters began to appear who seemed much better able to address it, like Alain Badiou and Jacques Rancière. The wheel turns."[4]

This transformation of the scene after Derrida and other postmodern philosophers left, as Critchley writes, represents a symptomatic change primarily in relation to the core postmodern patterns. Theorists of the end of postmodernism who are represented in the anthology of texts with the revealing title *Supplanting the Postmodern* acquaint us with the transformation of the scene in contemporary philosophy, art criticism, culture, and politics. Postmodernism evokes dissatisfaction, frustration, disappointment, and fatigue from the recycling of predictable approaches Raoul Eshelman).[5] This state of fatigue bring to mind the beginnings of the postmodern situation, as it was expressed by Lyotard in his texts on postmodernism. Fatigue from grand narratives or distrust of metanarration (Lyotard) is today replaced by fatigue from small narratives and the inability to distrust the grand narratives that sometimes transforms into fundamentalism (Alan Kirby).[6] Robin van den Akker, Timotheus Vermeulen, and other cultural theorists describe the transformation of artistic sensibility as the awakening of a sense of history and grand narratives, in connection with the crisis of liberal democracy, which no longer seems like "the end of history."[7] Critchley speaks of a revival of the idea of grand narratives in the works of contemporary philosophers. "The idea of the grand narrative has recently come back through certain theorists and artists. Sloterdijk, Braidotti, Ferry, Josh Toth, Nicolas Bourriaud, and 'The People of Seething'—a collective of people living in the London suburb of Surbiton, that was founded a few years ago so that they could write books and pamphlets, create videos, organize events, and which invented the founding myth of the Goat Boy who prophesied the seething—all of them are seeking to reintegrate the possibility of tomorrow into their conception of contemporary society, with the goal of overcoming and paralysis and even apathy, that the critical cynicism (the hopeful and boldly subversives sibling of cynicism) of some of their colleagues has turned into. However, when initiating these projects, they are aware from the beginning of the problems hidden in grand narratives. Sloderdijk warns that we should never derive conclusions from grand narratives."[8]

Another shift in the scene along these lines was visible in 2009, when the Birkbeck Institute for the Humanities in Great Britain organized a conference with the title "The Idea of Communism" at which Alain Badiou, Slavoj Žižek, Bruno Bosteels, Michael Hardt, Antonio Negri, Jacques Rancière, Alberto Toscano, Gianni Vattimo, and others presented. Jean-Luc Nancy was also supposed to participate. All the speakers, despite their different emphases, agreed that it is necessary to return a positive meaning to the idea of communism. Due to the extraordinary interest in the event, especially among young people, the organizing institution had to arrange for a theater hall with the capacity of holding a thousand people. The conference showed that the change in the intellectual atmosphere that Critchley had noted in 1999 had further intensified, and that communism as a word that symbolizes one of the main "grand narratives" had begun to evoke a certain enthusiasm among both the lecturers and the audience, even though at the beginning of the 1990s, the word had been pronounced dead.[9] An anthology was published from this groundbreaking conference, in which the outlines of the contemporary understanding of the idea of communism were established. This idea acts, at the very least, as a hypothetical possibility that it is possible to defeat capitalist exploitation and privatization approaches that are affecting an ever greater part of the commons. According to these thinkers, the idea of communism needs to be revived so that the idea of a society based on the inalienable connection between freedom and equality won't be lost from politics and political thinking.[10] It is significant that the idea of communism was also expressed in a positive manner by Gianni Vattimo, who—along with Derrida—is one of the postmodern thinkers who had been focusing his philosophy in this direction. Vattimo writes that it is essential to separate the idea of communism from metaphysical foundations used in the past, including laws of history, and also to decouple it from the industrialism that reigned in the former socialist countries. Vattimo links the idea of communism to his conception of "weak thinking," which expresses an anti-essentialist approach to social and political reality, and refuses the concept of a class as the "subject of change."[11] Slavoj Žižek has recently connected the idea of communism with the question of whether it's necessary to create global communism due to the entirely egoistic interest of surviving the global pandemic caused by Covid-19.[12]

Postmodern irony and cynicism give way to empathy and solidarity, the postmodern principle of play changes into a new seriousness, postmodern superficiality is replaced by a search for roots, the postmodern decentered and schizoid subject is abandoned in favor of new types of centered subject, authorship and autonomy, and the impossibility of truth is replaced by a longing for the existence of truths, the postmodern concept of uniqueness (singularity) is transformed into collective identities (the identity of a people, nation, class or certain local communities), radical plurality and multiplicity are connected with the search for new forms of unity. This list of transformations or replacements in postmodernism, which certainly is not complete, reveals concepts, stances, experiences and general cultural patterns that are emerging in the present situation. Studies of their emergence show that these patterns arise in relation to postmodernist patterns as a reaction to their exhaustion, but usually do not follow a radical detachment from postmodernism. As David Rudrum and Nicholas Stavris, who wrote the concluding essay in *Supplanting the Postmodern* argue, the end of postmodernism does not mean that a cultural turning point has been reached that would clearly separate the new cultural period from the previous one. We find here rather a gradual transition associated with apocalyptic events and situations at the beginning of the twenty-first century, such as the attack on the World Trade Center (WTC) (September 11, 2001), terrorism, the financial crisis, climate change, pandemics (SARS, Ebola, Covid-19), that evoke a ubiquitous "climate of anxiety."[13] Although emerging cultural patterns show signs of modernism (utopias, the autonomous subject, truth, unification, the work of aft), they are not separated from postmodern patterns by a radical act of negation that would call revolutionary change to mind. Most authors dealing with the current cultural situation agree that today's "modernism" is permeated with postmodernism and that emerging cultural forms give the impression of amalgams or hybrids that so far lack a corresponding concept, as Alan Kirby has emphasized. These units escape descriptions and terms that have their origin in postmodernism and modernism. The inadequacy of these descriptions and terms may be one of the reasons why in the present era, in a certain sense, a greater distrust of general concepts that are supposed to capture certain tendencies or epochs than there had been in the postmodern period, when—at least at a certain stage—there had been agreement on the use of the term postmodernism. Perhaps we can attribute this perceived inadequacy of general to the fact that those cultural formations are, in fact, truly *new*, even though they have both postmodern and modern traits. Their hybrid nature can be a certain appearance that arises because we apply the concepts that we've had so far at our disposal; that is, concepts from the repertoires of postmodernism, modernism, and in certain cases also premodern eras, as we have witnessed in the Identitarian movement, radical orthodoxy, and partially also in emancipatory social movements, as will be discussed later in the book. The new elements in contemporary cultural phenomena do not correspond either to postmodern concepts such as plurality, dispersal, deconstruction, singularity, or fragments, but they also don't correspond to the modernist concepts of unity, truth, the subject, or autonomy.

Hybridity and the Novelty of Contemporary Culture: Modernism and Postmodernism, and at the Same Time neither One nor the Other

The emerging forms can be described in two ways, but neither of them is satisfactory. They are both-and: they show both postmodern and modern traits. Therefore, some authors, such as Vermeulen and van den Akker use the typical expression "and at the same time." They formulate their description of the phenomenon as follows: contemporary romanticism expresses a desire and at the same time a skepticism toward the fulfillment of desire. However, we can also describe these formations through the connection neither-nor: these formations are neither modern nor postmodern. Neither of the conceptual repertoires offers us concepts that are able to satisfactorily capture the emerging formations. These two manners of description differ in the word structure both-and indicates the hybrid character of these formations (they are both postmodern and modern), whereas neither-nor expresses the fact that these structures are truly new, but we thus far lack adequate concepts to express them. Both of these manners of description are internally connected, because it's first necessary to describe these formations from the perspective of existing conceptual determinations; that is, in terms of the modern and postmodern conceptual repertoire, and only then is it possible to express the hypothesis that they are actually neither one nor the other. This collapse of the conceptual description heralds the *possible* presence of new elements that are not mere repetition or the result of mixing postmodern and modern patterns or codes. The presence of new elements can be understood as a hypothesis that we can only confirm indirectly through references to the discrepancy of the phenomena that appear here, and the existing conceptual repertoires. This recognition of the new in contemporary cultural formations takes the form of encircling phenomena with chains of negative definitions that have the character of a certain negation: it's not this. The phenomenon doesn't correspond to any concept and it is only similar or analogous to it. However, the use of the word structure neither-nor in itself is no guarantee that new elements are actually emerging here.

On the other hand, the renewal of modernist elements in a modified form does not mean that new elements are not emerging. As we know from the history of culture and art, in transitional periods or at the beginning of a new epoch, new forms of art appear by first making a certain return to the past cultural forms that offer the artistic means to express the new content, as was the case in the Renaissance. The restoration of antiquity in various artistic genres enabled the creation of works that were neither medieval nor ancient. An eloquent example is European opera, which arose in Florence at the end of the sixteenth century as a return to the principles of ancient Greek theater, as the dramatists, musicians, and philosophers of the time understood it. However, opera actually evolved from various musical forms that were scattered around Italy at the time, especially from the tradition of pastoral dramas with music.[14] These returns to the "plusquamperfect" that make up the "futurum" have their semantic logic, which we also find in contemporary culture. At its inception in early modern Europe, the opera acted as a hybrid ensemble form that cobbled together fragments from various traditions and historical periods, where many would seem not to belong together (Christian pastoral drama versus Aristotle's conception of Greek drama as one of the sources of inspiration for the origin of opera). The creators of the opera genre first had to distinguish their work from the musical genres that were cultivated at the time, as well as against the institutionalized tradition of church music that had been developing since the Middle Ages, and therefore they looked to ancient period as a "plusquamperfect" that preceded what appeared as the "perfectum" to these creators; that is, the recently closed past of medieval music. From their point of view, ancient drama belonged to the past, but it was perceived as a musical and dramatic form that enables the creation of a different formation, perhaps even incomparably different than anything that these artists and philosophers had encountered in Italy or Europe at that time. This new formation initially presented a hybrid impression because its creators could not base their work on historically authentic music from Greek dramas, which had only been preserved in a few small fragments which were almost entirely unknown in the period when opera originated. They therefore had to use existing musical forms and imprint them with their idea of ancient Greek drama. As it turned out, this hybrid form was actually a historically novel musical form that was not an imitation or repetition of an old form, but one that marked the beginning of four hundred years of the development of opera.

Contemporary cultural formations also cannot fail to be hybrid. The separation from postmodernism means that today's artists are returning to sources offered by modern and premodern culture. This return does not restore the modern or premodern state of culture in their real historical expressions, but it is an act through which contemporary artists use modern or premodern forms to create culture forms that will be different than postmodern ones. And these can be not only different, but also new, similar to the Florentine musical hybrid that was the start of the unique European phenomena of opera.

Given this hybrid nature of culture in the situation of transition or interregnum, we can divide cultural theorists according to whether both-and or neither-nor predominates in their description of these phenomena. However, this distinction cannot be strict. In today's culture, Vermeulen and van den Akker discover manifestations of a neo-Romanticism which appears in oscillation between postmodern irony and modern empathy, between postmodern distrust of utopias and modern desire for utopias, and so on.[15] In their conception of metamodernism, these authors conceive of contemporary culture as oscillations between postmodern and modern patterns, and their understanding of neo-Romanticism, according to which a longing for modern values is always undermined by postmodern skepticism and postmodern skepticism is dampened by the desire for modern values, which can be understood as the both-and structure. According to metamodernism, both postmodern aspects and modern phenomena appear in contemporary culture. However, this neo-Romanticism displays certain new features that we cannot find in the past, because these oscillations have never taken place between modernism and postmodernism before, only for the reason that they are taking place in relation to postmodernism as the culturally dominant paradigm of the last decades of the twentieth century, which means they are emerging after the end of a recently closed specific era. We can therefore understand metamodernism as something that is neither postmodernism nor modernism: neo-Romantic oscillations do not strictly correspond either to postmodern or modern patterns, and the term "neo-Romanticism" doesn't necessarily mean that some of today's art is directly related to historical forms of romanticism. We can find a similar connection between the hybrid structure of both-and with the innovative structure of neither-nor in practically all contemporary concepts of culture after the end of postmodernism. We can thus conceive of the definition of realism, as understood by Ihab Hassan or the Stuckists who will be discussed later, as a hybrid connection of postmodern and modern elements (the both-and structure) and at the same time also see in them a phenomenon that in the literal sense is neither postmodern nor modern (the neither-nor structure).

In the case of radical orthodoxy, we find that its representatives, such as John Milbank, do not respond to the emptiness of postmodernism with a certain modulated form of modernism, but regroup the meaning of individual cultural-social eras and flip the modernist idea of progress. According to their definition, premodernism is a culture in which there is a nonviolently arranged web of relationships among individual elements of being. Modernism disrupted this web, but was unable to create a new one and is therefore heading toward nihilism. Postmodernism is ambiguous: on the one hand, it's the culmination of modernism's nihilistic tendencies, and on the other it overturns modern secular reason with its universalist truth claims. With this subversion, postmodernism opens the path to the premodern and to creating premodern culture as a nonviolent web of relationships that Milbank calls an "ontology of peace." Radical orthodoxy had already embarked on this path at the beginning of the 1990s, which therefore makes it one of the first trends that was fully aware of the nihilistic consequences of postmodernism and crossed over its boundaries. Radical orthodoxy can be considered a trend that applied the both-and structure to postmodernism roughly ten years ahead of the other authors and trends mentioned when it performed its refinement and separated the nihilist part from the critical part, which makes it possible to break the universalist power of modern secular reason. Representatives of radical orthodoxy acknowledge the validity of this critical part of postmodernism, whose effectiveness in breaking the power of secular reason is much greater than the effectiveness of other critiques such as Bocheński's critique from the position of neo-Thomist logical rationalism. Authors who belong to the radical orthodox trend create conceptions using some postmodern patterns and approaches, as well as the premodern theological visions and values introduced by Augustine, Thomas Aquinas, and other theologians from late antiquity and the Middle Ages. In this way, the postmodern critique of modernism enabled Milbank and other representatives of radical orthodoxy to regroup the meaning of individual epochs so that premodernism is a culture of paramount importance, which we can only grasp thanks to postmodern philosophy, whereas modernism is a kind of historical detour or dead end. Postmodernism has opened the door through which St. Augustine and St. Thomas enter, dressed in the robes of deconstruction. Radical orthodoxy is unique in that, in a certain sense, it ironized postmodernism itself when it showed that Derrida and St. Augustine are thinkers who complement one another, as Milbank writes in his programmatic text "Postmodern Critical Augustinianism: A Short *Summa* in Forty-Two Responses to Unasked Questions."[16]

This structure of both-and (both postmodernism and premodernism) is associated with the structure of neither-nor in radical orthodoxy similarly as it is in current trends that arose after the end of postmodernism. John Milbank rejects the notion that premodernism means a return to the Middle Ages in the radical orthodox conception. Premodernism is a concept based on the postmodern critique of modernism, and it retains certain postmodern intentions, such as a nonviolent arrangement of relationships among elements. The concept of a postmodern premodernism that comes after the end of postmodernism is ambiguous: it contains the expression pre- with its semantic function of return, but at the same time it is also a certain manifestation. This is executed with a certain avant-garde gesture that attempts to establish an ontological vision of the nonviolent unity of being that must be realized in a terrain deformed by postmodernist nihilism. Premodernism in the concept of radical orthodoxy is neither a hierarchical nor a class-formed culture of the Middle Ages, nor is it a postmodern or a post-postmodern staging of the Middle Ages in which the characters of figures correspond to contemporary habits and ethical notions.

Alan Kirby, who was the most consistent in drawing attention to the inadequacy of existing conceptual repertoires, is the thinker who is probably best exemplifies use of the neither-nor interpretive structure. This author prefers the neither-nor interpretive structure, but is critical of the very phenomena that arise after the end of postmodernism. Kirby focuses on transforming subjectivity and textuality under the influence of digital technologies and the new social media. Phenomena arise that are not postmodern or modern—Kirby terms them pseudomodern or digimodern. In describing these variables the "current lexical state" fails, including words that are generally used today, such as nonlinearity and interactivity.[17] As Kirby shows, the postmodern "death of the author" appears to be a myth today. Digimodernism restores authorship in the form of creating internet blogs, Facebook statuses, or Wikipedia entries, but it is not modernist authorship that draws lines around creative acts related to an autonomous subject. Digimodernist authorship is becoming pluralist, as is clear in the creation of items on Wikipedia. However, according to Kirby, this pluralist authorship is not collective, because it is created in a hierarchical manner. In a digital medium, certain actors first introduce the initial parameters of the content structure and thus gain a higher position than the ones who in various times and places create texts that must adhere to the set parameters. Authorship has a differentiated form from the perspective of position, place, time, and number, but all the relevant actors can declare that they are authors.[18] However, the birth of a certain community of authors where a consciousness of joint authorship would be shaped does not take place here because authorship usually remains anonymous or encrypted. Authorship also no longer acts like Foucault's social sign. Digimodernist authorship is scattered among a number of zones and levels of fluctuating determinants, where its effects can be ubiquitous and dynamic or also covert, invisible, and not to be found anywhere.[19] As Kirby emphasizes, in digimodernist authorship the binary opposition of active and passive disappears. The author is no longer simply an active agent and the reader a passive consumer of text. The relationship between the individual and the text is so complex that binary oppositions fall apart when describing it. This relationship can be partially explained through the concept of intertextuality, but the expression "inter" evokes the incorrect impression that there is equality among the individual actors. This is because the activity takes place in a narrowly defined and predetermined sphere.[20] Kirby thus demonstrates that we do not find concepts in the existing repertoires that would do justice to digimodernist authorship. It is an activity that neither corresponds to the postmodern concept of the "death of the author," according to which authorship is a certain textual function, but it also isn't modernist authorship that is based on autonomous acts of human subjectivity. Digimodernist authorship is not only active but also must respect the predefined parameters and structures of the text, but it also isn't a merely passive reproduction of content. The notion of plurality and unity also fails, because authorship is neither the result of activity by a radically pluralist number of authors nor is it part of a process of their unification into a certain authorial collective identity. Kirby also finds the phenomenon of the failure of classification in other formations and manifestations, such as the digimodernist listener, publishing, and nonlinearity.[21]

Another author who, although to a lesser extent, also prefers the neither-nor structure is Nicolas Bourriaud. The idea of the archipelago that Bourriaud uses in his conception of altermodernism also appears in Deleuze, Guattari, and other postmodern authors.[22] However, Bourriaud adds a new meaning to it that alters its overall tone. "Archipelago" means a randomly created assemblage or constellation of elements in which originally isolated elements come into relationship and begin to act as elements of this constellation. An "archipelago" is a certain fluid whole without fundamental unity that lacks definition of its boundaries. Bourriaud conceives of this Deleuzean concept "alternatively" as a project of altermodernism that we bring into being when we make a modernist exodus from given traditions and temporalities. The "archipelago" is formed when we transform todays disordered plurality of isolated elements within it. Bourriaud claims that the "archipelago" is a model that encompasses all the dimensions of the present in their lines and perspectives. This model represents a constituted plurality of temporalities, complexities and chaos that is neither a petrified type of time that moves in loops and nodes (postmodernism), nor is it the linear temporality of modernism.[23] In Bourriaud's altermodernism we encounter the neither-nor structure that refers to the fact that the concept of the archipelago contains modernist elements: the will to reshape and to exodus, which are not entirely in keeping with the randomness that belongs to this Deleuzean concept. However, due to its postmodernist elements the altermodern concept of the archipelago also isn't a modernist concept. Bourriaud transforms the postmodern concept of the archipelago so that it becomes an intellectual model of "strategic universalism" in which an ineradicable semantic tension appears between unity and plurality that corresponds to this concept not being adequate either to postmodern patterns or to modernist ones. However, Bourriaud's understanding of the "archipelago" and "strategic universalism" at the same time shows that the neither-nor structure is in a relationship to the both-and structure. The concepts of the "archipelago" and "strategic universalism" has the postmodern significance of an assemblage of a multiplicity of elements without an organizing principle while also showing modernist traits because it's connected with a transforming unification.

In these theories and interpretations of contemporary culture and politics the interpretive structures of both-and as well as neither-nor always appear. Cultural theorists, according to whom the structure of both modernism (premodernism) and postmodernism predominate in contemporary cultural phenomena mainly perceive hybrid formations in these phenomena. The cultural theorists who prioritize neither modernism (premodernism) nor postmodernism in their interpretations emphasize that these phenomena are something new, even if we are unable to adequately express their novelty, because thus far we are still working with concepts and their combinations that were adequate to the past cultures. However, this multitude of names for the contemporary period in culture and politics is not necessarily due to the fact that we are only in its beginnings now. As will be further discussed later, this multiplicity of names can be ineradicable because we have entered the "pure" interregnum, in which the last semantic effects of the truth-events that enabled the creation of certain unifying names for the cultural period that was still termed "postmodernism" have ceased to operate.

The End of Communism and the Periodization of the Cultural Interregnum

After these introductory parts, in which I introduced the nature of today's reflection on culture after the end of postmodernism, I'm returning to the theory of the interregnum, which opens up a view on the present cultural situation in connection to the epicyclical model of postmodernism from the previous part. Several periodizations of the development of postmodernism and of its end appear in concepts and reflections on culture after the end of postmodernism. Needless to add that in the history of culture and art there is rarely agreement on the precise demarcation of the beginning and end of a particular period. However, theorists of the end of postmodernism mostly agree that the landmark in the development of postmodernism was 1989, and some even argue that this year heralded the end of postmodernism. John McGowan has brought forward the boldest political periodization of postmodernism, according to which postmodernism begins with the failed revolution in 1968 and ends with the revolutions in Central and Eastern Europe in 1989. In his interpretive intentions he agrees with Toth, whose ideas were discussed in the part of the book where I elaborated on the epicyclical model of postmodernism. Other theorists of the end of postmodernism also consider the end of the 1980s to be a cultural watershed in the development of postmodernism and the beginning of its end, although their interpretation of postmodernism does not exclusively relate to its political horizon. Besides Josh Toth, this list includes Linda Hutcheon, Ihab Hassan, Gilles Lipovetsky, Steven Connor, and John Milbank. I will be returning to some of their motifs later.

McGowan points out that in the works of Lyotard, Derrida, Foucault, and other postmodern philosophers there was the idea that an alternative to the liberal capitalist West exists. This idea fed their culturally revolutionary enthusiasm. According to McGowan, postmodernism was a project with colossal ambitions that attempted an overall reevaluation of the intellectual structures of Western culture and rejected its ethical and political consequences of colonialism, the dominance of market logic, and the politics of violence. In postmodern discourse we find the ideals of liberation and emancipation, which, although they had not been formulated explicitly, still acted as a shared political horizon. Postmodernism proclaimed itself to be a new culture that would carry out a liberating transformation of the foundations of European thought and culture. Postmodern philosophers have waged battles over crucial concepts in European culture, such as truth, reason, the subject, and the human being with the goals of proving that these concepts are not natural and of stripping them of pious worship. Their motive was to discover whether these "sacred" concepts were actually a hidden cause of the crimes committed by European civilization.[24] These ambitions were catalyzed by the ideals of the 1968 revolution, which, although it failed, had impulses that were possible to further develop at the level of theory and cultural practice. According to McGowan's interpretation, the year 1989 meant the end of these cultural-revolutionary ambitions in postmodernism. The disintegration and demise of the Easter bloc, which had embodied a certain alternative to liberal capitalism, represented the triumph of the West. As McGowan claims, if the oppressed people from the Eastern bloc identified with Western liberalism, then Western politics can no longer be considered an activity that rests on a rotten foundation that is necessary to subject to radical critique. The project of liberation and justice, which represented the postmodern theorists' political horizon has been put on the defensive. After 1989, a period arrived in which liberal democracy expands, as does capital, in the form of globalization. According to McGowan, the right is beginning to speak about great changes and revolutions, whereas the postmodern authors are abandoning their vision of any overall cultural and political transformation of the West, and they only believe in fragmented points of resistance. In his last texts, Derrida presents a vision of a new Enlightenment or even a new Internationale that would stop American power and capitalist globalization, but he is skeptical toward the possibility of overall cultural and political transformation. He also becomes skeptical toward the possibilities of deconstruction. In this later period he expresses a certain capitulation to Western metaphysics and violence when he admits that deconstruction cannot be extirpated, and therefore the only possibility is for deconstruction to be repeated again and again.[25] McGowan states that after the end of these postmodern visions of a total transformation of culture and politics there was then a tendency toward careful examination of subjects in detail, performed by sundry, disunified intellectual traditions. Gone are the days when a struggle was underway in philosophy over the fundamental concepts of European culture, science, and politics.[26]

Steven Connor distinguishes four stages in the history of postmodernism: accumulation, synthesis, autonomy, and dissipation. The accumulation stage took place in the 1970s and 1980s, when the hypothesis of postmodernism developed in various forms and in many disciplines. Postmodernist patterns were not stable then, and a more general conception of postmodernism was lacking. Mutually isolated concepts then began to be linked and synthesized in the mid-1980s. Frederic Jameson provided them with an authoritative synopsis and synthesis in his book *Postmodernism, or the Cultural Logic of Late Capitalism*. In addition, quite a few anthologies and synthesizing introductions to postmodernism also appeared: among these authors let us at least mention Thomas Docherty, Patricia Waughov, Charles Jenkcs, and Margaret Rose. Connor's periodization then became a certain barometer of the period and its cultural horizon in the second half of the 1980s and in the 1990s. Postmodernism expanded into the whole of society and created a generally accepted form of thinking and perceiving, or a structure of feeling (Williams). This was a stage in which postmodernism became a term for the cultural relativism that was widely bandied about in mass media and pop culture. Postmodernism became independent from the original objects of analysis (textuality), and began to freely associate with postcolonialism, multiculturalism and identity politics. Connor therefore speaks of an autonomous stage of postmodernism. It also indicates the increasingly unclear relationship between postmodernism as a description of a cultural situation and a certain project created by the founders of postmodern philosophy. In the last stage, due to its expansion and simplification, postmodernism begins to disintegrate and dissipate. The concept of postmodernism has become so indeterminate that it ceases to serve as a unifying conception that expresses particular cultural patterns.[27]

I presented a similar articulation of the history of postmodernism in the book *Cesty z postmodernismu* [Paths From Postmodernism], where I distinguish between early, peak, and late postmodernism. In early postmodernism I found the main feature to be an abstract or vague negation of unifying modernist universalism, and this was what made up its subversive side. In addition, I also wrote about the presence of technological and other euphorias. Thanks to the epicyclical model I am able to distinguish these traits of early modernism as core and peripheral patterns. And I also mentioned that the novelty of postmodernism was not pronounced. I dated 1989 as the beginning of peak postmodernism. During this period, postmodernism became academically institutionalized in Western countries. There is a rise in political particularism, which can be connected with a rejection of modernist universalism. This particularism sometimes takes a dark form, such as ethnic nationalism. Postmodernism lost its subversive dimension when it became an academic philosophy that is cultivated even in China. The postmodern manner of thinking, experiencing, and projecting has penetrated into politics, economics and all other social spheres and has been perceived as something natural that isn't necessary to thematize in any way. I mentioned postcommunist postmodernism, which, due to the politicization of life under state socialism, conceived of postmodernism entirely apolitically and didn't understand the political turn of Derrida's deconstruction. I connected the beginning of late postmodernism with the symbolic date of September 11, 2001, when the terrorist attack on the WTC was committed. This period saw the advent of a general politicization of postmodernism, which is manifested in the spread of postconceptual political art. As a result of the social naturalization of postmodernism, contradictions appear between its original emancipatory-subversive aspect and the use of postmodern patterns such as a critique of centralism or universalism in neoliberal politics or nationalism.[28] I created this periodization at about the same time when other periodizations of postmodernism appeared which were theorizing its end. What is valuable is that even though they arose independently of one another they display certain analogies. I have developed the motifs in these periodizations of postmodernism in this book into the theory of the interregnum.

1989 marks a decisive turning point in the history of postmodernism in all of these periodizations. McGowan views 1989 as the end of postmodernism, while Connor views it as the beginning of an autonomous stage of postmodernism that corresponds to what I have termed peak postmodernism. In these periodizations, 1989 heralds the beginning of a period in which postmodernism de facto loses its emancipatory-subversive significance. I consider this turning point to be a symbolic closing of the period of the extinction of the traces of radical emancipatory and modernist element thanks to which postmodernism had previously retained its subversive meaning. After this symbolic divide, postmodernism became the culture of the period of interregnum, whereas in the previous period it had still been drawing on the extinguishing elements that belonged to the closing sequence of the communist idea. At the end of the 1980s, Alain Badiou wrote about the paralysis of philosophy and the proclamation of its end: "Philosophy is then caught between the depletion of its historical possibility and the conceptless advent of a salvational turnabout. Contemporary philosophy combines the deconstruction of its past and the empty awaiting of its future."[29] Badiou sees postmodern philosophy as one of many forms of contemporary sophistry. This philosophy replaces the idea of truth with something else: with discursive operations, rules, language games, and references to the unspeakable.[30] According to Badiou, postmodern philosophy is moving toward historicism in the sense of accepting a given situation as the only possibility. The result is that philosophy accepts the parameters of the given situation as its own and involves one in "the normless disparity of discourses."[31] Through this move over to historicism, philosophy changes into sophistry and expels the idea of truth. Badiou claims the sophistic character of postmodern philosophy arose because it had been internally connected to historicism. However, it overlooks the fact that McGowan, Connor, Toth, and other theoreticians of the end of postmodernism write that postmodern authors related to the possibility of cultural and political transformation of the Western world, because they had held onto the impulses from 1968, or sometimes from other events, such as Foucault's case of the Iranian Revolution, and to a certain extent they respected the significance of the existence of the Eastern bloc as a certain barrier against capitalist globalization. Badiou states that from about 1965 to 1980 "obscure event elements" (événementialités obscures, Sylvain Lazarus) appeared in politics. We find them in the radical movement in 1968, in the Chinese Cultural Revolution, in the first state of the Iranian Revolution, and in the Polish Solidarity movement.[32] According to Badiou, these events do not have a clear name because their actors connected them with intellectual programs that have lost their effectiveness (for instance, May 1968 referred to Marxism-Leninism). Badiou sees this discrepancy as a sign that the work of naming them has not been completed. His reasoning on this can now be connected with the unclear naming of phenomena that arise in contemporary culture. Even their naming is not complete. Perhaps they contain ambiguous event elements that are insufficient for developing a truth procedure that would lead to a unifying name for them.

Based on McGowan's interpretation, postmodern philosophy can be understood as related to those political events which thus far every attempt made has failed at naming correctly. Perhaps their namelessness is one of the reasons why in postmodern philosophy distrust of the power of the signifier to name phenomena and events prevails. These vague event elements create a shared political horizon in their "namelessness" that fomented postmodern revolutionary ambitions, which McGowan claims concerned an overall transformation of culture and politics. In my opinion, this link between postmodern philosophy and ambiguous event elements explains why the postmodern philosophical enthusiasm ultimately dissipated: these ambiguous event elements didn't lead to a development of truth procedures that the postmodern enthusiasm could connect to. There was no truth procedure as a source for maintaining the enthusiasm in its original intensity. As we have seen when investigating postmodern euphoria, this type of affect did not disappear entirely from Derrida's philosophy, and it emerged in a metamorphosed form in his late period.

Mc Gowan's and Connor's analyses of the end of postmodernism can be reconciled with the theory of the cultural interregnum in my conception even though we differ in certain emphases. In their view, postmodern philosophy contains elements that relate to radically emancipatory visions. I emphasize that these radically emancipatory visions have a weakened or residual form, and that they are the extinguishing traces of political truth procedures that affect the peripheral patterns of postmodernism. The year 1989 marks the extinction of these traces connected with the sequence of the communist idea as we knew it in the twentieth century. This is the year when the cultural interregnum began, in which the peripheral patterns of postmodernism continued to operate, even though the source of their traces had been extinguished. However, they are in a state of becoming extinct and their intensity is tending to approach zero. For this reason as well, it is convenient to label them as peripheral. The model of the first period of the interregnum is an epicycloid that no longer has freely circulating "radicals" that interact with the elements that are part of it. its peripheral elements gradually became extinct and the second period of the interregnum arrived, whose origin we can date to the beginning of the new millennium. I focus on the fact that the peripheral patterns enable the development of the core formulas and that after the extinction of the peripheral patterns the character of the core patterns changes, as we will discussing in further subchapters.

The End of Postmodernism: Three Types of Explanation

Above, I have mentioned several distinctive periodizations of the history of postmodernism. In all of them, postmodernism is considered to no longer be a culturally dominant element. After 2000, proclamations of the end of postmodernism began to appear in cultural theory. Its end has been linked to various political, social, economic, and ecological phenomena that have given rise a feeling or conviction that postmodernism no longer expresses fundamental cultural and social dispositions and that it is necessary to create a new conception of culture and art. In contemporary cultural theory I find three types of explanation of the end of postmodernism.

The first type of explanation connects the end of postmodernism to the onset of capitalist globalization and the expansion and intensification of neoliberalism after 1989 (Nealon, Lipovetsky, Kirby). This explanation points to the economic absorption of postmodern patterns and their expansion into the body of society. According to Nealon, this is going on more intensively than it had been in the period when Jameson wrote about the phenomenon. Late capitalism from the period of the end of the Cold War changed into neoliberal "just-in-time capitalism," which intensified the individual targeting of marketing and maximized the flexibility and fluidity of the network of postmodern globalization.[33] Lipovetsky writes about the excessive intensification of previously existing structures. Hypercapitalism, a hypermarket, and hyperindividualism come into being. In the society this author calls hypermodern, hyperindividualism is the double of hypercapitalism. The individual seeks to maximize his or her profit, and disrupts previous social norms that regulated human behavior, and they manifest psychological disorders and extreme behavior.[34] Postmodernism disappears as a specific culture because its radical plurality, decentralization, and singularity were so interwoven with these excessive structures that they cannot be distinguished from one another. Through this permeation these patterns lose the specificity thanks to which it made sense to speak about a postmodern culture. In this type of explanation 1989 is understood as a certain turning point after which the influence of neoliberalism intensified and an expansion of capitalist globalization took place. Postmodernism became the "cultural logic" of hypercapitalism.

The second type of explanation of the end of postmodernism relates to the social expansion of postmodern patterns (Connor) and their institutionalization

(Hutcheon, Connor, Kirby). This second type of explanation can be set into relation with the previous explanation, even when the authors mentioned do not address the connection between the expansion and institutionalization or postmodern patterns and the development of neoliberalism and capitalist globalization. There was an institutionalization of postmodern patterns such as decentralized subjectivity, disruption of dualities, irony, and play. Institutionalized postmodern schemes then cannot capture new phenomena that escape them as Raoul Eshelman writes.[35] Postmodernism is an academic power. Academics making a living from the institutional practice of postmodernism have a tendency to overlook these phenomena and to pretend they don't exist.

This type of explanation specifies the effect that was caused by the decay of peripheral patterns. Postmodernism without traces of subversive emancipatory practices becomes repetitive and schematic. Its approaches and conclusions repeat with increasing frequency like institutionalized schemes. The result of the extinction of peripheral patterns is fatigue from the endless repetition of the same approaches: disrupt the boundaries between styles, deconstruct, decenter, ironize, call everything a cultural construct, and so on. There are reasons why postmodernism should be replaced by something different.

The third type of explanation is offered, for example, by Nicholas Stavris, who, as one of the editors of the *Supplanting the Postmodern* anthology, depicts the general social mood at the beginning of the twenty-first century. Society is experiencing ubiquitous anxiety and uncertainty over the present and future, economic crisis, climatic changes, and religious fundamentalism, and it is witnessing apocalyptic events: the attack on the WTC on September 11, 2001, terrorism, wars, and global pandemics. The times are much harder than they were in the period when postmodernism originated and dark clouds fill the horizon.[36] In 2017 Vermeulen and van den Akker also wrote about the political phenomena that shape contemporary sensibility: new social movements, right-wing populism, a loss of confidence in neoliberal globalization, and the disintegration of the project of a united Europe.[37]

This type of explanation points out that postmodernism, with its playfulness, freedom from commitments, and irony is unable to express the contemporary social mood or structure of experience. The term "structure of experience" comes from Raymond Williams, and Jameson used it in his analysis of postmodernism. Robin van den Akker and Timotheus Vermeulen then used it again in their investigation of culture after the end of postmodernism. They understand the structure of experience as an element that defines culture, but it isn't possible to identify it with any of its individual admixtures. The structure of experience "expresses the way in which a certain period or generation—ironic, anxious—can differ from another generation, serious and full of hope. [. . .] as soon as this structure changes, new means are perceived as necessary and feasible, while old means begin to appear empty and artificial."[38] A certain structure of experience works in various movements, styles, and individual cultural expressions, but without the phenomenon representing a specific exemplary form. Van den Akker and Vermeulen provide examples taken from various expressions that arose in differing contexts, genres, and rhetorical logic as examples where a sense of truthfulness and hope appear, such as Barack Obama's "Yes We Can" speech, filmy labeled as "quirky" (Wes Anderson and Miranda July), "freak folk" (CocoRosie and Devendra Banhart) and the "new sincerity" literary trend inspired by David Foster Wallace's writing.[39]

We can generalize van den Akker and Vermeulen's description of the structure of experience so that a change in the structure of experience occurs after patterns that express the postmodern structure of experience become ideologies because their peripheral patterns have been extinguished (for instance, subversively emancipatory intentions), and this is what maintained them at least at a minimal distance from institutions and the economic system. This new structure of experience arises alongside the postmodern patterns or in opposition to them and it's formed by anxieties, political and civilizational insecurity, apocalyptic events, and the hardness of the times (Stavris). The names of the artistic trends and theoretical initiatives that emerge after the end of postmodernism bear witness that these phenomena born of the crisis and apocalypse of the contemporary world are analogous to the phenomena the modernist structure of experience grew out of (the First World war as a military apocalypse, the disintegration of the empires of the age, the economic crisis of 1929). Re-modernism, alter-modernism, meta-modernism, and other names of these initiatives are not only a way out of the conceptual helplessness after the emptying of postmodern concepts, but express the structure of experience which is formed by similar phenomena to the ones that shaped modernism. The desire for another world, authenticity, seriousness, empathy, enthusiasm, hope, and other patterns that contemporary art theorists find in today's culture corresponds to a different type of experiencing the world than the one that corresponds to postmodernism with its playfulness, non-commitment, and irony. However, the postmodern patterns are still active, as most theorists of the end of postmodernism admit, seemingly paradoxically. We can explain this presence of postmodernism after it was no longer a dominant cultural element through the fact that no new truth-event has emerged in either art of politics that would create its one name and its own generic procedure. In other words, there is no event and subsequent truth procedure that would have the same significance that the birth of cubism and abstract painting or the Russian Revolution of 1917 had for modernism. We now find ourselves in the second period of the interregnum, when a number of artistic and political trends and theoretical initiatives arise, from which—on principle—a unifying name for the present situation cannot be derived. Postmodernism was this unifying name because it related to modernism with its truth procedures which created the unifying naming of the artistic trends. This is evidenced by its defining adjective "post." In the interregnum the new structure of experience is often again named through the word modernism, but now it is already too historically distant, and therefore its name doesn't evoke a unifying idea. The starting point for naming the current cultural situation is ultimately the cultural and political formations in which the various postmodern, modern, and premodern patterns intertwine. However, these formations are inadequate to the task of giving us a name that will be taken as a unifying label for the contemporary situation after the end of postmodernism.

The Prosthetic Character of Postmodernism

The epicyclic model of the relationship between postmodernist and modernist patterns can now be supported by two theses. The first thesis states that in postmodernism, modernism is present in various modifications and is held by many cultural theorists (McGowan, Hutcheon, Rancière, Toth, Wellmer, and others). The second thesis states that if these patterns weaken and become extinct, it means the end of postmodernism. This is a thesis that we find presented in various forms by Toth, McGowan, and certain others. Toth speaks of a spectral existence of modernist patterns, which are necessary so that deconstruction has its conditions of both possibility and impossibility. McGown discovered a similar dependence of postmodern patterns on modernist political patterns (the existence of political and economic alternatives). We can essentially find this thesis in its implicit form in all the theorists who connect the end of postmodernism with the evaporation of the last traces of the political, social, and cultural projects connected with the culture of modernism. It testifies to the prosthetic character of postmodernism, which is analogous to the prosthetic nature of neoliberalism. Postmodernism requires prostheses in order to develop its patterns. In the period when it arose it was supported by peripheral patterns that are dependent on the presence of the traces of emancipatory and modernist procedures. After the extinction of these trace and the subsequent extinction of the peripheral patterns, postmodernism was no longer "pure." It's linked in principle with any value system, political trend, or economic doctrine since the application and development of postmodern patterns depends on "external" values, conceptions, and visions as its prostheses: in this sense, postmodernism is promiscuous. Later we will see the various things it has been linking up with.

The example of Derrida's philosophy shows that the core pattern of the pluralist operations of deconstruction has the idea of absolute justice as its peripheral pattern, and this is the undeconstructable condition of deconstruction. However, the idea of absolute justice is only effectual in deconstruction when Marx's spirit or spirits, representing the possibility and impossibility of communism as absolute justice toward the individual, appear(s) on the horizon. I understand Derrida's communist horizon as an expression of the fact that in society there are still traces of communist event elements with "unclear names," mainly the final reverberations in politics and culture of the radical emancipatory dimension of 1968. After 1989 these traces definitively become extinct, and Derrida presciently recognizes that without them the idea of absolute justice itself becomes incomprehensible or is also extinguished. However, the idea of absolute justice is the condition for deconstruction. Therefore, Derrida realizes that for the sake of the future of deconstruction it is necessary both to evoke Marx's spirit and to maintain the horizon of messianism without a Messiah, which means the possibility and impossibility of a society in which absolute justice to the singular (communism) exists. If we interpret this approach in relation to the elliptical model, it means that Derrida was aware of the meaning of the peripheral pattern (absolute justice to the singular) for the core pattern itself; that is, for deconstruction. The core formula remains the core when a peripheral formula acts upon it, which itself is conditioned by a radical emancipatory political horizon with a low intensity. I conceive of this horizon as the presence of extinguishing traces of communist event elements (the spirit of 1968). With this approach, Derrida offers testimony that postmodernism has a prosthetic character.

The Elliptical Theory of the End of Postmodernism

Let us now formulate what follows from the thesis of the prosthetic character of postmodernism in the situation that arises after the extinction of the peripheral patterns of postmodernism in the period after 1989. According to this thesis, their extinction will result in a change of the character of the postmodernist patterns. In the epicycloid model, the transformation of postmodernist core patterns takes place after the eccentric external motion induced by the peripheral patterns has ceased. This change can be described as a mutation of core formulas that leads to a change in the position of the postmodernist patterns. Below, we will see several examples of how this mutation takes place. Instead of modernist peripheral patterns related to the traces of truth procedures, patterns appear that connected, for instance, to the functioning of institutional art, or to real political strategies (metapopulism), or even to a protofascist horizon (the Identitarian movement) appear. The postmodernist patterns themselves do not impose any constraints on the ideas, strategies, and horizons that might intersect with them. Postmodernism has a promiscuous character, which will be discussed later. The mutation of postmodernist patterns occurs when their peripheral patterns, which had lent them an emancipatory and subversive direction of development have been extinguished. However, due to their prosthetic nature, postmodernist patterns have to connect to some other patterns. They are no longer associated with the emancipatory, subversive patterns that defined the direction of their development, so nothing prevents them from linking up with ideas, strategies, and horizons that contradict the emancipatory, subversive character of the original postmodernism. Their connection with artistic and academic institutions, with conservative populist strategies, or with neoliberal capitalism changes the character of the postmodernist patterns. I term this character change a mutation of postmodernism.

The position of postmodernist patterns changes as these patterns lose their place in the center of the cultural formation and come to occupy one of two points that each have the same significance for the production the given formation. This is because postmodernist patterns are connected with ideas, strategies, institutions, and horizons that then determine the direction of their development. As we will see using the example of the Identitarian movement, the use of the postmodernist patterns of plurality or uniqueness corresponds to a certain culturally neofascist vision of society that is a relevant guide here. Although this vision is changing due to the influence of postmodernist patterns, the postmodernist patterns are no longer central. There are therefore two focal points: the given requirement, idea, or vision (e.g., the institutional requirement of an academic or artistic operation or an Identitarian vision of a cultural community) and the postmodernist patterns. Various cultural and political formations are emerging whose production has the character of circulations around two foci, neither of which represents the center. These circulations can be represented as an ellipse, which will be introduced in more detail later.

The change in the position of postmodernist patterns, in which these patterns cease to be the core patterns means that postmodernism loses its dominant position and it means the end of the culture that has been called postmodernist. The mutation of postmodernist patterns because of the extinction of peripheral modernist patterns leads to the disappearance of their dominant position. Their position is no longer in the core, but in one of the two focal points in the ellipse. This is how I explain the phenomenon that is called the "end of postmodernism" in cultural theory. It is an explanation based on the prosthetic nature of postmodernism and it's linked to the interpretations of the end of postmodernism in contemporary cultural theory that were discussed above. This explanation provides a theoretical model that we'll call the elliptical theory of the end of postmodernism. It captures the processes that took place during the first period of the cultural interregnum (1989–2000) and led to the beginning of its second period, which arrived after the end of postmodernism.

For the sake of completeness, it should be added that the peripheral patterns of postmodernism have not entirely disappeared. There is no annihilation of peripheral elements, but only their extinction, which can be understood as their annulment. By this, I mean the fact that the intensity of their action tended to decrease to zero. Metaphorically speaking, their annulment had occurred, but this didn't necessarily mean their complete annihilation. We can still find their emptied forms that express a null or empty set, which in mathematics is understood as a condition of all sets with extensions greater than zero. The peripheral patterns of postmodernism do not disappear entirely, because we encounter them throughout the entire period of the interregnum, at a minimum in the form of empty signifiers. After 1989, subversive and emancipatory expressions in culture and society gradually became precisely these empty signifiers. Their intensity had diminished to such an extent that they are unable to affect the postmodernist patterns, but they continue to exist as signs, emblems, or words emptied of content, as evidenced by the use of the word "revolution" in the advertising industry. Later, these empty signifiers of political and cultural modernism become forms that enable a crystallization of contents that will form certain patterns called meta-modernist, re-modernist, alter-modernist, or pseudo-modernist.

Institutional and NeoliberalMutations of Postmodernism

Let's now look at a few examples of the mutation of postmodernism: cultural-institutional, neoliberal, and Identitarian, and we will devote the most attention to the last one, which represents a phenomenon that is both relatively new and also clearly demonstrates the promiscuous character of postmodernism. I'm leaving the institutional and neoliberal mutations without further elaboration because I've already dealt with the institutionalization of postmodernism and neoliberalism above. As previously stated, Hutcheon, Eshelman, and others have written about postmodernism becoming an academic power and losing its avant-garde ambitions and subversive positions. Academic and artistic institutionalized postmodernism turned deconstruction, the disruption of dualities, the decentered subject, and contextuality into a repetitive template which lacked the ability to react to new, emerging phenomena. Stavris and van den Akker and Vermeulen point out that postmodernism no longer expresses society's present disposition. According to these authors, a structure of experience is coming into being in now that is different than the postmodern structure, but in the academic world they are still usually working under the assumption that nothing has changed and that most of society continues to think, experience, and manifest itself in the same ways as postmodern society had. In this case, postmodernist patterns mutate into templates or even conceptual fetishes that are unable to express new tendencies in art and in society. More specifically, they obscure or downplay the significance of these tendencies and create the impression that the dispositions of art and society are the same as after 1989. Thus, the ideological mutation of postmodernist patterns has taken place.

Another type of the mutation of neoliberalism is neoliberal mutation. Above, we have seen that according to Boltanský and Chiapello, a new spirit of capitalism began to appear in the beginning of the 1970s, which was effective because it absorbed the anti-hierarchical elements of 1968 and turned them to its managerial and capitalist uses. This new spirit of capitalism gradually found its cultural and philosophical expression in the conceptions of deconstruction, dispersal, decentralization, and antiessentialism that make up the core pattern of postmodernism. Many social scientists and philosophers have noticed this interrelationship between postmodern culture and neoliberal or flexible capitalism. Here, let us name David Harvey, Fredrik Jameson, Alex Callinicos, Terry Eagleton, Richard Sennett, and Michel Vakaloulis. In my works that discuss the paths of postmodernism I have emphasized precisely this mutual interlinkage between postmodernism and the new spirit of capitalism, but in this book I pay more attention to the avant-garde and subversively emancipatory elements of postmodernism that relate to the political horizon left as a legacy from 1968. The social expansion of postmodernism in the 1980s and 1990s that Connor writes about took place as an expansion of a conformist type of postmodernism that was detached from the subversively emancipatory peripheral patterns. In its place, a postmodernism that had nothing to do with this radically emancipatory political horizon spread. It detached itself from these peripheral patterns and linked up with neoliberal patterns. As a result, there was a social expansion of postmodernism and postmodernism then became ubiquitous. As Brown writes, postmodern patterns mutated in such a way that they became a symbolic or cultural expression of neoliberal practices. The individualization of responsibility corresponds to the mutated pattern of singularity. The neoliberal practice strengthens the "uniqueness" of human capital, which after the collapse of the egalitarian function of the invisible hand of the market and the principle of merit accepts the principle of the radical randomness of profit and the absence of economic justice. The randomness of profit in the present phase of neoliberalism is a mutated form of postmodern radical randomness that disrupts any instance of order, including the spontaneous order that was created by the invisible hand of the market. The neoliberal decentralization of competencies can be understood as a mutated pattern of decentralization that belongs to the core postmodern patterns. This pattern was tied to the anti-hierarchical impulse of 1968, when the principle of equality and justice were developed. Once decentralization and antihierarchicalism detached themselves from the peripheral pattern of equality and justice, they smoothly integrated with neoliberalism, in which they mutated into a form that causes stress and anxiety, or else apathy, as Brown writes. We can interpret the decentralization of competencies as the postmodern pattern of decentralization that mutated when it connected with neoliberal rationality and capitalist imperatives.

We have seen how postmodernist patterns mutated in academic and art institutions and how they mutated in neoliberalism. In the first case, they became a set of schematic procedures or templates, and in the second case they transformed into cultural ciphers of neoliberal practices. These mutations have caused deconstruction, the disruption of binaries, contextuality, singularity and decentralization to take on an ideological rotation that is in tension or even in contradiction with the ways Derrida, Lyotard, Deleuze, Foucault, and other postmodern philosophers understood their concepts and approaches, and their subversively emancipatory effects were replaced with ideological effects. However, the Identitarian movement shows us an even more striking example of this.

Identitarian Mutations of Postmodernism (The Identitarian Movement and Alain de Benoist)

Identitarian politics and theory are a relatively recent movement that often entirely consciously and deliberately uses postmodern patterns, especially the patterns of multiplicity, diversity, plurality, uniqueness (singularity), and alterity. Ihab Hassan writes that the need for multiplicity, plurality, and diversity was caused by the crisis of modernist and traditional identities. However, instead of respect for others, this identity crisis led to fundamentalism and new forms of tribalism. According to Hassan, after the end of the great narratives there have been scattered and fragmentary micronarratives that cause a weakening and loss of the sense for the public sphere. In this way, the foundations of civil society start falling apart and its disintegration into smaller and smaller self-centered identities accelerates.[40] Hassan indirectly testifies that postmodern multiplicity, plurality, and diversity were originally connected with respect for others (in Derrida's conception, as we discussed above). However, this respect for others did not expand. the pattern of multiplicity, plurality, and diversity lost its peripheral pattern and a mutation occurred in which instead of respect for others, self-centering tendencies that aim at establishing a difference between "us" and "them." The pattern of multiplicity is then no longer bound to respect for others, because it creates an image of radical others who have heterogeneous value systems. Self-centered communities recognized the right to radical otherness and the plurality associated with it: they justify their attitudes, values, and emotions, no matter how prejudicial, irrational, or hateful by saying that they are radically different or alternative. The term "alt-right" that was adopted by the new radical conservative movement in the United State and Europe takes advantages of this function of the word "alternative." Instead of using historically burdened terms such as neo-Nazism, anti-Semitism, or racism, this movement refers to the idea of radical otherness. Derrida's concept of alterity, which in the period of postmodernism's expansion and increasing autonomy was emptied out and disconnected from its emancipatory charge, has mutated into a pattern that serve as a legitimation strategy for the radical conservative movement. The alt-right movement uses slogans such as "going against the mainstream" in order to further strengthen its alternative character, inspired by the leftist and ecological movements of the 1990s and the early post-Millennial years, such as the alter-globalization movement.[41]

The alt-right is a wide-branching movement that includes the pan-European Generation Identity movement, which distances itself from racism as expressed by their slogan "0% racism, 100% identity."[42] It also opposes chauvinism, xenophobia, and neo-Nazism. At the same time, the Generation Identity movement rejects the contemporary form of liberal democracy and demands a direct and *organic* democracy, which can be achieved in a society composed of communities with political participation and their own cultural identity. The Identitarian movement had its beginnings in France in the late 1960s when it started to take shape around the authors of the New Right (Nouvelle Droite) and the GRECE group (Alain de Benoist, Guillaume Fayet, Dominique Venner). The next-generation Identitarian movement arose in France in 2012, when they occupied a mosque that was under construction in Poitiers and proclaimed their demand for a nationwide referendum on banning Islam in France and halting migration. The Generation Identity movement has turned against the generation of 1968, which they see as responsible for the dismal present condition in Europe, and they refuse their hedonistic individualism, egotistical careerism, liberalism, and multiculturalism, which allegedly disrupted European culture and caused a feeling of rootlessness among young people.[43] The 1968 generation is blamed for having the main share of responsibility for today's young people living in stressful conditions, subjected to social and cultural uncertainty, and lacking a life perspective and value orientation points. In his book *Generation Identity: A Declaration of War Against the '69ers*, which represents a kind of militant manifesto for the movement, Markus Willinger writes about apathy, despair, burnout, promiscuity, and drugs as the young generation's reaction to the hopeless situation they have to live in.[44] According to the manifesto, Europe lost its authenticity because the 1968 generation had unilaterally focused on revealing violence, oppression, colonialism, and other crimes. European identity was something to be suspected and rejected. The result of this total critique was that European identity fell apart and an individualism permeated with hedonistic nihilism or egotistical careerism spread. European society changed into a collection of egotistical individuals without identity.

Markus Willinger paints an unflattering portrait of the 1968 generation, which, due to their liberal individualism, failed on all fronts: in family life, in childrearing, in politics, and in economics. Liberal democracy is deeply corrupt, and multiculturalism has created a society of communities that hate one another. Young people have to work much more than the previous generations and they have only minimal chances for social advancement. Although the 1968 generation spoke about economic growth and prosperity, it only provided economic well-being for itself, and not for the young generation, who will have to pay their debts in a crumbling economy. And while the older generation often speaks about ecology, it hasn't managed to introduce any structures that will avert an ecological catastrophe. Willinger sums up the 1968 generation as having led Europe to the brink of suicide.

Willinger wants to speak for his entire generation and he calls on young people to embrace their European heritage and develop an authentic European identity. He invokes the ideas of ethnopluralism, cultural diversity, and respect for foreign cultures. We also read in his manifesto that non-European cultures are threatened by the import of a false modernity and arrogant application of progress and human rights from the West. The Generation Identity movement endeavors to preserve the "proud and ancient cultures of India, China, Russia, Persia, and many other countries," that are being exposed to crusades for universal human rights and supposed progress. Willinger and the Generation Identity movement follow the French New Right and the theoretical group GRECE, where it has borrowed its main ideas. The GRECE group has applied certain postmodern patterns to create the Identitarian political philosophy, which transcends the established definitions of political trends. Just the disruption of boundaries between artistic genres is a typical pattern in postmodern art, the abolition of boundaries between right-wing conservatism, fascism, Marxism, and the postmodern left is typical for the New Right.

The most relevant representative of this group is Alain de Benoist, whose work is called a historically new form of fascism by some critics.[45] However, other authors refuse to identify him too closely with fascism, and point out that de Benoist's conception of identity is not homogenous, but dialogical.[46] The fact that de Benoist also publishes his essays in the magazine *Telos*, which subscribes to the tradition of critical theory (the Frankfurt School) and to nondogmatic Marxism also testifies to a deep breaching of the boundaries between political and intellectual movements.[47] His critical engagement against neoliberalism, capitalist globalization, and Americanization is similar to Derrida's Baudrillard's or the contemporary representatives of leftist thought. In the 1980s, de Benoist distanced himself from the conservative right, which had adopted the free market and globalization paradigms. In this period, he also opposed Le Pen's National Front because he disagreed with their narrowly defined nationalism and defense of economic.[48] De Benoist arrives with his own conception of communitarianism that he contrasts with neoliberal capitalism, state-centralized democracy, globalization, and Eurocentric universalism. His conception is reminiscent of radical democratic communitarianism when we observe how he writes about communities with the greatest participation of citizens in political decisions in the form of city councils, regional assemblies, professional associations, "grass-root" initiatives, and other community formations.[49] These communities are the foundation of the organic democracy that will overcome the present crisis of democracy dominated by technologies of power and where the content and value assumptions of democracy are falling apart.[50] De Benoist advocates the autonomy of all ethnic and cultural identities and refuses the institution of the centralized nation state as the expression of Jacobin thinking. He favors a federalized European Union based on principles of subsidiarity and ethnopluralism, in which individual communities (ethnic, linguistic, gender) are the basic political units that represent non-territorial associations of people on the basis of their choice.[51] It opposes the racism and xenophobia of ultra-right-wing groups and movements, because this phenomenon ultimately damages their own cultural identity. This criticism of nationalism and racism is connected to the central concept in his theory, which is ethnopluralism.

De Benoist states that we are in a period of decline, in which European culture is in mortal danger, and that non-European cultures are also in a similar danger. Like Heidegger and Adorno, he is also seeking the beginnings of this critical state deep in the past, and he finds them in the emergence of Judeo-Christian monotheism, which laid the foundations of egalitarian universalism that later developed into the Enlightenment and Marxism. In particular, the Enlightenment, modernism, and capitalism spread to all the large cultures, where they caused cultural homogenization. This progressive homogenization of the world, which had already appeared two or three thousand years ago, is intensifying in the modern world to such an extent that cultures are losing their uniqueness and specific spiritual ideas on which social existence are based.[52] According to de Benoist, the pre-Christian cultures of Europe show us authentic cultures whose uniqueness wasn't suppressed by egalitarian universalism, and their paganism can be partially renewed even today. It is necessary to discover the "metarational foundations of the ideational and organic civilizations of ancient Europe."[53] According to de Benoist, sometimes a total cultural decolonization takes place even in the contemporary world, which frees a particular culture from the influence of European universalism and returns its freedom and independence. An example of a cultural decolonization of this type is the Iranian Revolution in 1978, which Foucault had also understood in a similar spirit as de Benoist.[54]

De Benoist has an ambiguous relationship to Marxism and to contemporary leftist theory. While he sees Marxism as a source of egalitarian universalist politics, at the same time he also appreciates the Marxist critique of capitalism, because he sees one of the main dangers for the preservation of a multiplicity of cultures in the global hegemony of capital. The way he puts it is that although he isn't a Marxist, he agrees with Marx about some things. He acknowledges the effects of class contradictions, but he considers the main conflict of our age to be the conflict between the "new ruling class" and "the people." De Benoist takes inspiration from contemporary leftist sociologists, such as Christopher Lasch, and he even translated works by several contemporary Marxist authors into French. He considers the ecological crisis as another serious threat and calls for support for ecologically oriented policies that would lead to a reduction of consumption and to negative growth (degrowth).[55]

De Benoist refuses universalism as such, and replaces it with the concept of diversity derived from postmodern philosophy. He also approaches multiculturalism from the perspective of preserving cultural diversity. In his opinion, multiculturalism is failing because it leads to mixing cultures, which destroys their diversity and causes their homogenization. The reaction to this homogenization is communities enclosing themselves in "multicultural ghettoes."[56] Insurmountable barriers of prejudices and hateful emotions arise between communities, and cause damage within them. De Benoist criticizes multiculturalism in the name of cultural diversity, which is a condition of multiculturalism as a policy that recognizes a multiplicity of cultures. In his view, diversity and the preservation of a radical plurality of cultures justifies the application of the concept of ethnodifferentialism or ethnopluralism. This should replace all forms of universalism and become a policy that confronts multiculturalism and its homogenization. De Benoist bases this idea in the incommensurability and heterogeneity of individual cultures, but he does not attribute any unchanging essence to them. He uses the postmodern concept of identity, which is established in the process of differentiation, and understands cultural identity as a process of defining itself against different cultural identities. Cultural identity arises as a reflexive self-formation in relation to a system of cultural differences. According to de Benoist, this process is conditioned by the existence of certain dividing lines between cultures. This is the way he drives the need to recognize different cultural identities. A unique cultural identity can only develop if different cultural identities are present. European identity can only be reestablished if there are also Chinese, Indian, Arab, and African identities. However, it is necessary for the different cultures to be as unique and distinct as possible. This can be achieved in two ways. First, Europe should stop its human rights crusades so that different cultures can develop authentically and radically differently. This will initiate the process of differentiation that will lead to a reestablishment of European culture. Second, it is necessary to activate the communities of immigrants in Europe to return to their own cultural environment so they won't lose their cultural identity.[57] De Benoist justifies cultural exclusion through the postmodern concepts of diversity, radical plurality, and singularity, and through critiques of universalism. We also find a certain idea of equality here. According to de Benoist, all cultures are equal on principle and none of them can make a claim to universal superiority. A horizontal and mutual respect should emerge, along with recognition of differences that at least preserves the present state of the given cultures.[58]

De Benoist's conception of ethnodifferentialism is reminiscent of fascism or national socialism because it calls for a certain cleansing of foreign elements from the European cultural space, but by contrast with these historical forms of politics, it does not create myths that would serve as a foundation for cultural identity, such as the German myth of "blood and soil." If we accept the term fascism as a definition of thinking and of politics that attempts to exclude foreign elements from a given space, de Benoist's fascism is non-essential, because it isn't based in a collection of predefined values. It is a fascism justified by certain core postmodern patterns. Although it is based in part on authors who had always inspired conservative or fascist thinking, their work is sifted through conceptual filters made from postmodern philosophy. In her book *The Politics of Postmodernism* Linda Hutcheon describes the deconstruction of essentialist thinking as a postmodern tool for critiquing undemocratic or racist and fascist politics.[59] However, in de Benoist's philosophy and in the Identitarian movement, the deconstruction of essentialism and universalism become tools of fascism. Ramón Flecha has documented a new type of fascist discourse that draws from postmodern thought using the example of Identitarian populist politicians, such as Jörg Haider. Haider never described the Turks or Moroccans living in Austria as a racially or culturally inferior group of people: he only claimed that they were different, and he said he felt friendly toward them.[60]

De Benoist criticizes the universalism of human rights in a way strikingly similar to the way Deleuze had. He considers human rights to be an abstract mechanism of Western civilization that suppresses cultural differences based in the immanent life of the given culture. Human rights postulate the existence of a "universal human nature independent of historical periods or places that is recognizable through reason." This abstract nature causes three separations: human beings are separated from other living beings (they are merely the holders of natural rights), from society (the human being is an individual for whom society does not play a role), and also from the cosmic whole (human nature does not owe anything to the general order of things).[61] Deleuze is critical of human rights because he considers them a transcendence that is the product of immanence that negates itself. Human rights say nothing about the "immanent modes of existence of the people who are their bearers."[62] Deleuze refuses to think about human rights independently of the "games" of neoliberal capitalism. He understands human rights as an essential part of its "games" and adds that there is no democratic state that isn't deeply compromised by its contributions to creating human suffering. Deleuze's main objection to human rights is that they "assume a universal and abstract subject of rights, which isn't possible to identify with anyone specific and translated into individual, real-life personalizations."[63] We can also hear echoes of Marx's distinction of man as an abstract citizen and a specific human being embedded in real social relations in de Benoist's work. For both thinkers, human rights are an object of criticism because their universalism creates an abstract subject that separates human beings from individual forms of life and culture that are part of a specific period and social space. De Benoist and Deleuze criticize human rights due to the immanent understanding of the human being and cultural phenomena that relate to a horizontal development of diversity and singularity.

Miranda Christou sums up the current debate about the appropriation of the postmodern concept of difference by the New Right by describing the concept of difference as a boomerang that was sent out by postmodern thinkers and is now returning in a racist form. She mentions Ramón Flecha, who writes about the penetration of "differential racism" into anti-racist pedagogy, which fixates on the struggle against biological racism, but unwittingly uses differential racist arguments by continually repeating that every culture is distinct and none is superior to any others. This extreme relativism is an effective means of dissolving universalist moral and political principles. Miranda Christou considers this combination of difference and universalism to be the main challenge posed by postmodern racism.[64] However, the universalism he has in mind is the universalism of human rights, democracy, and humanism, which de Benoist associates with an abstract conception of the human being and global domination by capital. This form of universalism is proving to be intertwined in many aspects and in many countries with the mechanisms of European and American hegemony, and therefore it can be assumed that it won't be possible to add on the postmodern concepts of diversity, singularity, and radical plurality. Miranda Christou poses the question of how to free postmodern concepts from the fascist political horizon and connect them with human rights, democracy, and humanism.

This question itself is further proof that postmodernist patterns have a prosthetic character and they will always require certain concepts, strategies, and horizons in order to be brought into effect, no matter where they come from.

The Postmodern-neofascist Horizon of the Identitarian Movement

Willinger and the Generation Identity movement declared war against the '68ers. We know that Derrida, Deleuze, and Lyotard follow the subversively emancipatory ideas of 1968; that is, they belong to the '68ers, but despite this, the Identitarian movement uses their concepts. This clear contradiction in relation to the '68ers can be explained by the fact that de Benoist, Willinger, and other representatives of the Identitarian movement adopt postmodern patterns, but without taking on their radically emancipatory horizon, which had definitively faded away in 1989. De Benoist, Willinger, and other Identitarians linked them to a radically conservative or even fascist political horizon, and from Willinger's words we can deduce why. He claims that today's young generation is drawn to the idea of cultural identity for the same reason that young people espoused the left in 1968 and the right in 1933.[65] It's because of the emptiness and nihilism of the system in Western Europe and the United State before 1968, and in Germany before 1933. Willinger and the young Identitarians cannot accept the leftist or communist political horizon as the young generation had in 1968, because they associate it with universalist demands that they claim have caused the catastrophic state in Europe and the world. They make a slapdash connection of the 1968 movement's political horizon with the universalism of human rights as a means to suppress different cultures. However, they fail to discover the universalism of the communist idea, which differs from the universalism of human rights precisely in that its subject is a specific human being in real social relations, and not an abstract being. Although de Benoist appreciates Marx's critique of the abstract human being, he doesn't believe in the possibility of universalism, in being able to overcome separation from other human beings, from society, and from the cosmic order. According to Badiou's typology of subjects, we could classify de Benoist's approach to the reactive subject category, which doesn't connect to a certain truth-event and creates an intellectual apparatus of "reactionary novelties."[66] Nevertheless, May 1968 still represents a "nameless" event that has an unclear generic procedure. Its communist elements gradually became extinct and in the political and cultural space they ceased to operate as a formative and distinguishing factor. The empty place that remained after them was filled with the universalism of human rights.[67] As a result of their absence, Willinger and the Generation Identity movement identify the universalism of human rights with the universalism that was active in 1968, and because of this switch, they reject the universalist elements from 1968. They then adopt Derrida's, Deleuze's, and Lyotard's conceptions without their implicit communist horizon, which they are unable to recognize. Therefore, they are using postmodernist concepts and approaches like free radicals that can connect with radically conservative values. However, after this connection there is a mutation of the postmodernist patterns because they have taken on a different direction of development than they had when they were still connected with the peripheral modernist elements surrounded by the radically emancipatory horizon. The direction of their development was determined by radically conservative values and an implicit fascist horizon. People are beginning to perceive them differently than they had in the 1970s and 1980s. They appear with increasing frequency in the strategies and speeches of Identitarian and conservative populist politicians, and this changes the way we experience postmodernist patterns. Postmodernist patterns enable the Identitarians and conservative populist politicians to make their political opponents confused and insecure. The postmodernist patterns helped them breach the boundaries between conservatism and the left and the boundaries between democracy and fascism. When we examine de Benoist, Willinger, and Identitarian movements, it raises the question of how we can even define the contemporary political field, when the Identitarian movements and the postmodern part of the radical left are more in agreement in certain formative patterns than the Identitarian movements match the traditional right-wing parties, and more than the postmodern left matches traditional left-wing parties.[68] Examples of these common patterns are, for instance, the rejection of European universalism as the suppression of cultural diversity, criticism of Eurocentrism, and the superiority of cultural identity over class identity.

The Identitarian movement spreading the ideas of ethnodifferentialism and ethnopluralism is a formation that's typical for the present stage of the interregnum in the sense that it's impossible to adequately label and categorize groups using established concepts such as right, left, conservatism, democracy, and fascism. Each of these concepts shows its inadequacy, because the Identitarian movement develops concepts that are neither exclusively from the right or the left, or exclusively conservative, and so on. They are at the same time right-wing in some aspects, and left-wing in others, and also conservative, democratic, and also even fascist. We would hardly find the idea of ethnodifferentialism in historical forms of fascism, because it relates to the postmodern idea of radical plurality and difference as conditions for every definition. It does not apply to a nation or a nation state, but rather to a community that is defined non-essentially. A consensus is lacking in discussions about ethnodifferentialism and ethnopluralism in the Identitarian movement on whether these formations are a mere camouflage for revived racist and fascist movements, or if instead they are a historically new form of thought and politics that contains intellectual patterns associated with fascism and Nazism (exclusion, purifying the community, an organic society, closedness), while also contradicting some of the old movements' other patterns (biological racism, the centralized state, the inferiority of different ethnic groups). The Identitarian movement takes over certain elements of the radical left and ecological movements (criticism of capitalism, decentralization, direct democracy, cooperation between communities, the idea of degrowth/negative growth), and it even creates its own internationale.[69] The political horizon of the Identitarian movement are communities that develop their own authentic cultural values, free from the allegedly destructive effects of foreign cultural elements. This horizon follows the fascist notion of the harmonious development of nations that cleanse themselves from disruptive and corrosive elements such as Jews, socialists, and communists, who came as the bearers of cosmopolitanism internationalism, and radical universalism. The Identitarian political horizon has fascist roots, but it is distinguished from historical fascism by its postmodern strategies. Therefore it can be called postmodern fascism.

The Identitarian movement provides a wide range of mutations of postmodernist patterns. Difference mutates into ethnodifferentialism, plurality mutates into ethnopluralism, singularity changes into the uniqueness of cultural values, the critique of universalism changes into a principled rejection of universalism because it's alleged to destroy communities' authenticity. These postmodernist core patterns lose their position as the central point, because they're in relationship with radically conservative or neofascist patterns that define how they are applied. Evidence that the postmodernist patterns have lost their central position is the fact that the Identitarian movement explicitly rejects some of these patterns. After all, it is primarily the postmodernist mixing of styles, genres, and cultures which the Identitarians believe is harmful and which they must fight against. This is because mixing cultures is in irreconcilable conflict with their neofascist horizon of authentic cultures. The Identitarian movement has a high evidentiary value for the character of postmodernism. It provides clear evidence that after the loss of its radically emancipatory horizon, postmodernism can be combined with any kinds of demands, strategies, and horizons, and even perhaps with a radically conservative or neofascist horizon. The Identitarian movement eloquently testifies to the promiscuous character of postmodernism in the period of the interregnum.

The Promiscuity of Postmodernism

I have provided three examples of mutations of postmodernist patterns: institutional, neoliberal, and Identitarian mutations. There are many more similar examples—there is also the form of contemporary populism that I call metapopulism, which will be discussed below. In its Russian variant we meet with political strategies that explicitly draw on the concepts and approaches developed by Lyotard, Baudrillard, Deleuze, and other postmodern philosophers. Russian metapopulism became influential because its ideology and practical approaches use postmodernist patterns such as a radical plurality of rhetorical games or "truths" in combination with patters of various kinds: conservative, neoliberal, Keynesian, militarist, Orthodox Christian, and socialist. As we see from these examples, postmodernist patterns after the extinction of their peripheral patterns, which were bound to traces of communist, modernist, or avant-garde elements will connect with de facto any kind of political or economic ideology. It can even be an ideology whose goals are opposed to radically emancipatory ideals, such as neofascist ideology. After the extinction of its subversively emancipatory and modernist peripheral patterns, postmodernism behaves promiscuously. It can be connected with political liberalism, post-Marxism (Mouffe and Laclau), populism, military strategies, ultraconservatism, neofascism, Medieval theology ("radical Orthodoxy")—and the list could go on.

This promiscuity is due to the fact that postmodernism arose as a collection of concepts and approaches whose trajectory of development did not emerge from them themselves, but was instead defined by the subversively emancipatory patterns in the peripheral positions that were tied to political and cultural notions and practices from 1968 and to their consequences. As soon as their traces burned out and the entire previous radically emancipatory horizon disappeared after 1989, its subversively emancipatory peripheral patterns also gradually disappeared. As has already been stated, these patterns defined the subversively emancipatory direction of development of the postmodernist patterns, and as soon as they were extinguished, the postmodernist patterns found themselves in a vacuum of values. However, according to the thesis of the prosthetic character of postmodernism, postmodernism is never "pure," because the nature of its patterns is such that "external" values, conceptions, and visions are necessary for their development. The postmodernist principles themselves—differentiation, dispersal, decentralization, disruption of boundaries, and so on—require at least some text, some intellectual territory, genre, style, work of art, in which they can be applied. They cannot be applied by themselves to themselves. At the same time, this always happens in certain social, political, and economic contexts that affect the course of differentiation, dispersal, and so on, and influence or even determine the direction of their progress. It is generally true that postmodernism cannot exist without a social context.

Once its peripheral patterns burn out, modernism loses is original political and value orientation and finds itself in a condition where in principle it can be linked to any kind of values, conceptions, and visions at all. Due to its prosthetic character it seems to offer itself up to connection with anything that enables it to prolong its life. Its prosthetic character causes its promiscuity. Postmodernism cannot be promiscuous once the last traces of the communist idea and of modernism have been extinguished. This promiscuity results in postmodern patterns mutating into forms that are determined by the values, conceptions, and visions that are connected with postmodernism. Its promiscuity means that postmodern patterns no longer occupy a core position in the intellectual, political, and other formations that arise in the present interregnum. They relate to patterns that have the same position of significance they have, or even a more significant one, because they determine the selectin of postmodernist patterns, as we have seen in the example of the Identitarians who refused postmodern mixing of cultures. As soon as postmodernist patterns lose their dominant position, a situation of "the end of postmodernism" arises, as was discussed in the subchapter "The elliptical theory of the end of postmodernism." The cultural and political formations that emerge after the end of postmodernism are therefore formations in which we find postmodernist patterns that have mutated into forms corresponding to the concepts, vision, and ideologies that have connected with them. We will become better acquainted with these formations below.

What Comes after the End of Postmodernism? Cultural and Political Formations of the Present Stage of the Interregnum

The formations that appear in the present stage of the interregnum act as a flood of phenomena that bring innumerable various tendencies, imitations, references, and connections. It's not easy to create any systematic overview that would capture their similarities and approaches to creating new styles. This is not only because these formations are arising, so to speak, right before our eyes over the period of the last twenty years—that is, since the year 2000, which represents the symbolic end of postmodernism. The reason for this lack of clarity is also the very nature of these formations, which evade established classifications. As was discussed in the introductory subchapters of this part of the book, these are formations that are both postmodernist and modernist, and at the same time they are neither postmodernist, nor modernist. Nor does contemporary cultural theory provide a systematic overview, because each author focuses on a somewhat different type of phenomena or they create such phenomena themselves. Among other reasons, this is also because they only follow the changes in some of the postmodernist patterns and use different criteria for evaluation. However, despite all the differences, we at least see a tendency toward naming similar phenomena. This common tendency expresses the fact that many theories of contemporary culture and of emerging artistic trends use the name modernism along with a certain delimiting prefix, as we have seen at the beginning of this part of the book (remodernism, altermodernism, metamodernism, etc.). However, other theoreticians or artistic trends choose different names (performatism, renewalism, Stuckism), so there is no consensus here over whether contemporary art can be characterized using the word modernism, even if it's modified with a prefix.

Therefore, I present only a selected overview of the formations that appear in the domain of art and art criticism, in the domain of cultural theory, and in the domains of theology and politics. In them, we find mutated postmodernist patterns, hybrid connections of "incompatible" elements, compositional assemblages, returns to premodern forms of thinking and religion, and starts made toward new truth-events. Despite all the chaos, confusion, and contradictions in contemporary culture and politics let us take note that in individuals formations there are certain general traits. Later, we will illustrate them by using the model of an ellipse.

The Domain of Art: Remodernism, Stuckism, and Radical Realism

In the domain of art, we encounter a growing awareness of changes in the manners of thinking, perceiving, and expressing that had previously sought clearer and more compact concepts and artistic expression. The American art critic Jerry Salz, as well as many others, noted changes in artistic sensibility that are manifested in installations and objects exhibited in galleries in the United States and in Europe. Postmodern irony and a cool distance are no longer the dominant manner of expression; however, they haven't disappeared, but instead have been connected with sincerity and enthusiasm. The curator Tanja Wagner writes about exhibition where we encounter oscillations between melancholy and hope, between apathy and empathy, between fragmentation and wholeness, ambiguity and purity. The art critic Jörg Heiser claims that the rational and calculated conceptual art of Jeff Koons or Cindy Sherman is gradually replaced by affective and sometimes sentimental abstraction of artists like Tacita Dean, Didier Courbot, and Mona Hatoum. He describes this trend as a romantic conceptualism where the point is not deconstruction, but rather reconstruction.[70] David Rudrum recognize the advent of authenticity, earnestness, and spirituality, which weakens or even replaces the postmodern shibboleth of irony. As he states, there are common themes in contemporary art, which appear in various genres and styles, so it isn't easy to determine what, exactly, they have in common.[71]

We find the gesture of negating postmodernism in Stuckism and remodernism, which was founded by the British artists Billy Childish and Charles Thomson, who promulgated the "Stuckist Manifesto" (1999) and the conceptual statement "Remodernism" (2000).[72] They understand Stuckism as the first artistic trend that belongs to remodernism, which is their term for a rebirth or renaissance of modernism. An artistic gesture of rejecting postmodernism appeared in their statements earlier than it had elsewhere. These statements express a protest against postmodernism, which had become orthodoxy and establishment.

Conceptual artists such as Damien Hirst regularly collect art awards and exhibit in prestigious galleries, and their works sell for high prices to influential institutions and corporations. Postmodern art is sponsored both by conservatives and Labor Party politicians. In their statements we read that the postmodern artists' connection with the political and economic establishment makes a mockery of these artists acting as though they are subversive and avant-garde. Stuckism and remodernism are a reaction to the institutional mutation of postmodernism in the arts that was described above. The authors of these statements openly speak about the bankruptcy of postmodernism and the ossification of its patterns and practices. They oppose conceptualism, hedonism, and ego-artists, and declare the end of irony, pastiche, parody, and bricolage. The Stuckists return to the first generation of modernists, especially Kandinsky and Eliot, where they find the qualities, attitudes, and positions needed for overcoming postmodernism. They discovered a new meaning for authenticity, earnestness, beauty, skill, and spirituality. The Stuckists reject the nihilism of postmodern art and take inspiration from the first modernists who considered authentic soul-searching to be the condition of art. Stuckism considers itself to be the first artistic trend that is following the modernist impulses that were disrupted and suppressed by postmodernism. They announce a return to realistic painting, which serves them as a medium that enables self-recognition in relation to reality. Against the fragmentation of experience and the separation of sense and sensibility, the Stuckists subscribe to the renewal of artistic sense for the whole, in which sense and sensibility, conscious and unconscious, signifier and signified act in mutual interrelationship. By doing this, the wealth and spiritual depth of human experience that was distorted and torn into pieces by postmodern art will be restored. According to the Stuckists, new worlds are created through painting and unknown psychological realities are entered which the individual—thanks to the medium of painting—experiences along with others.

There are certain tones in Stuckism and remodernism that are reminiscent of premodern artistic and theological postulates. Stuckist are does not seek what is new, but instead that which is eternal. It recognizes the authority of tradition and absorbs "eternal" principles that express the wisdom and knowledge of all of humanity. Remodernism is not just concerned with the rebirth of the modern, but also with the rebirth of spiritual art. It turns to a spirituality that brings the soul to Earth and exposes people to a truth that exists independently of the desires and ideas of the human individual. Remodernism proclaims that spiritual art restores the true relationships between people as well as relations between people and the Divine. Spiritual art grows out of an awareness that